TAPESTRY OF LIFE
BOOK II

Devotions for the Unique Woman

Presented To
∞

From
∞

Date
∞

TAPESTRY OF LIFE

BOOK II

Devotions for the Unique Woman

by

Nancy Corbett Cole

Tulsa, Oklahoma

Tapestry of Life Book II: Devotions for the Unique Woman
ISBN 1-56292-286-6
Copyright ©1995 by Nancy Corbett Cole
Edwin Louis Cole Ministries
International Headquarters
P. O. Box 610588
Dallas, Texas 75261

Published by Honor Books
P.O. Box 55388
Tulsa, Oklahoma 74155

Contents

7

Dedication

To my loving husband, Edwin.

Acknowledgments

I want to thank my friends and family for enriching and enlarging my experience and enjoyment of life. I especially want to thank my sisters, Ellen, Patsy, and Brenda, my brother Jimmy and his wife Elaine, and their families; the Welebas, Conlans, and Tates; the Whartons and Garrisons; and my dear friends Ruth Jones, Lucy Hollison, Hilda Dimancheff, Betty Powers, and Marlene Ostrom. You are the gold threads in the tapestry I call my life.

I also want to thank my daughter Joann Webster for her literary and organizational skills in helping me assemble these thoughts into a concise and readable book, and express my deepest gratitude to the editorial staff of Honor Books for their hard work and expertise.

And, of course, I must thank those whose lives are intimately interwoven in mine: my children and grandchildren, Paul, Judi, Lindsay, Brandon, Bryce, Lois, Rick, Holland, Kendal, Richard, Josh, and Seth.

Introduction

Every woman takes the threads and materials each day hands her and works them into the tapestry that becomes her life. When the mature woman looks back, she may either see the beautifully patterned masterpiece God intended for her, or she may see a frayed, chaotic fabric that strayed from the Master's design.

If the tapestry of your life is fraught with imperfections and loose threads, it can be rewoven by placing it in the hands of your Creator. God can transform a tattered life by reweaving the threads submitted to Him and making something wonderful and precious from them. He can bring beauty from ashes and miraculously change the most undesirable tapestry into an extraordinary piece of art.

In this book, I have described the life experiences of myself and those around me. The pattern of each woman's life is unique — no two designs are exactly the same — but one common thread we can share is the love of our Savior, Jesus Christ. He enables us to be overcomers and conquerors. He can mend any flaw. He can enhance any life.

I pray the words in this book will speak to your heart. I believe God can transform the common threads of your daily life into a glorious tapestry, a masterpiece of His design.

Strands of the Soul

ONE

Live!

My friend Sherry sighed deeply. She was trying to enjoy her birthday dinner, but it was the hardest one she had ever attended. At thirty-one, she felt like her life was almost over. Sharing her special day was difficult even for her friends.

As I gazed at Sherry's distraught face, I thought of my friend Honey, who probably cannot even remember her thirty-first birthday! Still, I've never heard her complain. When she isn't accompanied by an aging man whom she calls her husband, I doubt anyone would be able to guess her age—even though she must be in her seventies.

I had spoken with Honey by phone just a few weeks ago. "Let's go to the art museum," she said. "Let's put our lives on hold for a couple of hours!" What a great idea! I don't know when I last went to the art museum.

Honey is the type of person to think of something like that, and just the friend I'd love to spend time with at a museum. She is one of those people who seems to make every day into a party. She remembers to do special things for herself and others even when it's no one's birthday. She lives to make each day memorable, enjoyable and invigorating.

Some people, like my young friend Sherry, give up too easily on themselves and on life. There's no reason to sigh at age thirty-one, fifty-one or even seventy-one! Life is how you find it where you are. There are new experiences, friendships and ways to enjoy each day and decade. So don't get bogged down in worries or regrets. Live, like Honey, right where you are.

The bottom line is: Live!

MEDITATION:

"I came that you might have life, and have it more abundantly" John 10:10 (author's paraphrase).

ACTION STEPS:

🐦 When was the last time you did something just for the sheer enjoyment of it? Do it *now!* Spend the next hour pampering yourself. Take a long soothing bubble bath, or rub your body with scented lotion and lay down for a nap.

🐦 Call a friend and ask them to do something they wouldn't normally do for themselves. Perhaps you know someone like me who doesn't always think of things I can do for myself. I was thrilled Honey called me. I'm sure you have a friend who feels the same. Even if you just do each others' nails, any special treat makes life more enjoyable.

🐦 Name the next year of your life. Prepare for your next birthday by thinking ahead what age you'll be. Envision all the great things you can do with that year of living. Then name that year. Call it the "Year of Authority" or "Year of Wisdom" or something else you highly value. Once you're in it, live accordingly!

LIFE·GIVERS :

"I still want to do my work, I still want to do my livingness. And I have lived. I have been fulfilled. I recognized what I had, and I never sold it short. And I ain't through yet!"

Louise Nevelson
Artist

"In spite of the cost of living, it's still popular."

Kathleen Norris
Writer

LET'S PRAY :

Father, thank You for this gift of life. In Your presence is fullness of joy—help me each day to express Your love and share Your joy with those You bring into my life, in Jesus' wonderful name I ask this. Amen.

Cheerfulness:

During one period of my marriage my husband seemed to change overnight, and I found myself constantly responding to him negatively. I thought he was terribly irksome. I was certain it was him, not me. I was right and he was wrong. Period.

Then I read this proverb: "A wise woman builds her house. A foolish woman tears it down with her hands." God's Word arrested me and let me know I was tearing down my own household by my negative words. It was as if God spoke to me, "Be wise Nancy; *build* your house."

The Bible says, "A merry heart doeth good like a medicine" (Proverbs 17:22). Negative attitudes can cause sickness, both physical and mental, but cheeriness will actually hasten the road to health. And cheeriness builds and uplifts all those around you.

Cheerfulness is a choice.

The Apostle Paul was falsely accused. Bound by chains, he told the Roman governor, "I cheerfully answer for myself!" (See Acts 24:10.) I read that and thought, *Cheerfully! Why wasn't he upset?* Later Paul and Silas sang and praised the Lord until God miraculously released them from prison.

Paul was cheery because he knew God was with him, for him, and in him. As a result, despair simply couldn't gain a foothold in his life. God is on our side too! We never need to wallow in the negatives of life, nor impose them on others. We can be the cheeriest people on earth.

When I realized my error, I adjusted my attitude, and immediately my husband seemed to change too! Overnight, his quirks and foibles became so minor as to be of no consequence to me.

I had been tearing down my house. It was me, not him! My negative attitude had been detrimental to me as well as to those closest to me. If God had not stopped me, it could have become a habit of pessimism that would have affected my family's health and happiness. When I was in this attitude, it was difficult for me to think differently or recognize what I was doing.

Thank God I heard His Word of discipline and committed myself to focus on the positives. As soon as I did this, my household began to be restored.

MEDITATIONS:

"He who finds a wife finds a good thing, and obtains favor from the Lord." Proverbs 18:22 RSV

"A merry heart doeth good like a medicine" Proverbs 17:22

"As he thinketh in his heart, so is he" Proverbs 23:7

"Be renewed in the spirit of your mind" Ephesians 4:23

ACTION STEPS:

❧ Begin today to reprogram your mind to be positive. Read God's Word daily. It is the absolute best way to change your thought life.

❧ If you are habitually negative, start looking at the foods you eat. Are they what is best for you? Chemical imbalances and food allergies can make people think the whole world is against them or that only bad things happen to them.

❧ Get proper rest and enough relaxation. Fatigue can take away cheerfulness, and being a slave to a routine can take all the fun out of life. If it's not possible to get away from the house, at least get a good book or a hobby you want to develop.

❧ Do you have trouble deciding if you're overly negative or just "realistic"? Ask for input from someone close to you, especially your spouse. You may hate the answer, but sometimes bitter medicines cure best.

❧ Bitterness, unexpressed grief and other spiritual strongholds can create negative attitudes. A good Christian friend, a trained counselor or a Christian twelve-step program (now offered in many churches) may help you discard the negative and focus on the positive.

SOMETHING TO QUOTE EACH DAY:

God is *in* me.
God is *with* me.
God is *for* me.

WISE WORDS:

"A happy woman is one who has no cares at all; a cheerful woman is one who has cares but doesn't let them get her down."
                                        Beverly Sills
                                        Singer

"Misfortune, and recited misfortune in especial, may be prolonged to that point where it ceases to excite pity and arouses only irritation."
                                        Dorothy Parker
                                        Humorist, Writer

Aging:

We may not always feel like it, but getting older has its benefits. A recent university study revealed that people find more satisfaction in later decades of life than in their youth. When I thought about those surprising results, I understood why.

Thinking back, I remember the excruciating pain I felt in early years at an embarrassing moment or when I blundered into a humiliating faux pas. The survey listed those awkward, insecure teen years as the hardest. Being older and wiser now, I have enough confidence to feel secure in nearly any situation, especially with God anchoring me.

Remember the decisions and questions that used to haunt our youth? When I was eighteen years old, I asked a young friend who had just married, "How do you know what real love is?" I did not have a clue then. Now I can answer that question, for I have experienced love. I no longer wonder who I am going to marry. God gave me a husband who turned into a wonderful, compassionate and loving Christian man.

I also know how many children I will have. And I know their names, personalities, skills, talents, whether they'll go to college, who they'll marry, and what they'll do for a living. I know what my career is and approximately how much money I'll make, where I'll live and what my lifestyle will be.

Thinking of all that, it seems obvious that our later years should be the most satisfying. Although we still have to keep our minds and bodies as active as possible, we can at least relax in who we are.

So whether or not you feel like it today, accept this period of your life as the best ever. Treat it like that, and it will be.

ACTION STEPS:

❧ Take a minute to relax in who you are. Sit back and reflect on who you have become. Remember the bad times, and congratulate yourself on surviving them and learning from them.

❧ If you are given to regrets and tormented by the woulda-coulda-shoulda blues, make yourself a memory book. Put pictures or thoughts of all the good things that have happened in your life—a famous person's autograph that you got, a program from a play you saw, a canceled airline ticket or brochure from your favorite vacation, or any awards you may have received. Then, when you're tempted to remember the decisions you've blown or the opportunities you've missed, thumb through the pages. Remember all the times when you made the right decision, took the opportunities, wore the right dress, or were in the right place at the right time.

WISE WORDS:

"Yesterday is a canceled check; tomorrow is a promissory note; today is the only cash you have—so spend it wisely."
Kay Lyons

"Perhaps one has to be very old before one learns how to be amused rather than shocked."
Pearl S. Buck
Author

"Old age is no place for sissies."
Bette Davis
Actress

$\mathscr{P}$atience:

This year I reread the story of Noah in Genesis, chapters 5-7, and had the uncommon experience of every sentence of this familiar passage springing to life. It was like a fresh story. Noah was a real person and, surprisingly, his story helped me to understand myself.

Noah and his wife were ordinary people who worked hard and raised a family. Then one day God spoke to Noah and instructed him to build a very large ship. As he built this huge boat, he and his wife were ridiculed because there had never been rain or flooding on the earth. For over one hundred years he worked on it, and they patiently waited for God to vindicate them.

Finally the ship was completed and, at God's direction, Noah brought in the animals. God closed the door and the rain began to fall. The couple had little time to feel the comfort of being justified. They were stuck on a ship, bobbing around on flood waters, with hundreds of animals and their grown children cramped in tight quarters.

Eventually the ark rested on dry ground as the flood waters receded. But it was months before God allowed them to leave their temporary home. What patience!

Each of my grown children has come back to live in my home for varying periods of time. I know that many times any of us could have erupted with an impatient comment or have become exasperated with the situation. However, in dealing with my life and family today, whenever I'm impatient I think of Noah and his wife! They withstood incredible difficulties that make mine look small.

Impatience is the root of most tensions in both the home and workplace. More arguments begin in the home through impatience than anything else. Thinking, "I've had it," and letting words fly is never the best action, no matter how justified you may believe you are.

The next time you're tempted to fly off the handle and say things you'll regret, or give up on something before you've seen its fulfillment, remember Noah and his wife and their patience. They endured and saw God's promise become reality.

MEDITATION:

"I waited patiently for the Lord and He inclined unto me and heard my cry." Psalm 40:1

ACTION STEPS:

๕ Running out of patience ruins relationships. One of the best self-improvement courses you can give yourself is to look for an opportunity to practice patience every day.

๕ Relax before you act. The old adage, "Count to ten before you speak," is still a good one. Some reports now claim that part of our stress and overreaction to it come from not properly oxygenating our brain cells through deep breathing. While you are patiently counting, breathe deeply ten times.

WAIT 'TIL YOU HEAR:

"You take people as far as they will go, not as far as you would like them to go."

Jeannette Rankin
U. S. Congresswoman

LET'S PRAY:

Father, let Your patience have its perfect work in my life and give me the ability to recognize each situation as an opportunity to allow Your grace to grow in me, that I may be perfect and whole, wanting nothing. Thank You for Your loving patience with me. In Jesus' name I pray. Amen.

Maturing:

N o woman I know likes to think she is old. I have always been quite active, so I really didn't think too much about my age. That is, until the day I met it face to face in my favorite grocery store.

I was working my way down an aisle when our paths crossed. He was a cute little boy sitting in a shopping cart. I glanced at him. His bright eyes met mine and without hesitation he blurted out, "You're a grandma!"

Now, I loved being a grandmother from the minute my first grandchild was born. But I never thought I looked like one! My moment of truth came from the lips of a five-year-old boy.

Right then, I knew I had crossed that indistinct yet very real line that marks the end of youthfulness. I was now wearing the garment of maturity. Like years ago when someone first called me "Ma'am," the response of a stranger reflected my age better than my own mirror.

But isn't it strange that even though we mature in many ways, we still remain basically the same person we were when we were teenagers? We still think in the same patterns, react to people in the same way, have the same sense of humor and occasionally succumb to the same old bad habits.

I am annoyed with myself when I fall back into a lifelong habit that I was certain I had overcome. I look in the mirror and say, "Nancy, you may be mature on the outside, but on the inside you have never been rid of that same ugly thing!" Thank God, those times are fewer and fewer as He continues to fashion within me a new person made in His image.

However many years I have left, I want to continue becoming better and better. I want to live to the fullest, learn the most, experience great joy, and influence others. I especially want to be able to give an answer to anyone at any time about the hope that is within me through knowing and serving God.

MEDITATIONS:

"O death, where is thy sting? O grave, where is thy victory? The sting of death is sin...But thanks be to God, which giveth us the victory through our Lord Jesus Christ." 1 Corinthians 15:55-57

"And God shall wipe away all tears from their eyes; and there shall be no more death." Revelation 21:4

ACTION STEPS:

&❧ Looking back on your life, when was the greatest time you had alone with God? Have you tried to duplicate that recently? When I first became a Christian, people told me to "pray through" about things. That meant you prayed until you received an answer from God, or until you knew that He was moving in your behalf. How about setting aside some time today to "pray through" or just be alone with God? Those are usually the happiest and most peaceful times we have on earth, giving us a glimmer of what we'll have in heaven.

WISDOM OF THE AGES:

"Come to me in the silence of the night;
Come in the speaking silence of a dream;
Come with soft rounded cheeks and eyes as bright
As sunlight on a stream;
Come back in tears,
O memory, hope, love of finished years."
"Echo"

Christina Rossetti[1]
Poet

JUST FOR FUN:

*"Perhaps one has to be very old before one learns how to be amused
rather than shocked."*

Pearl S. Buck
Author

Integrity:

In a celebrated news story, a mother with a fifteen-year-old son admitted her involvement in a twenty-year-old bank robbery and turned herself over to the police. She said she had experienced grief, depression and suicidal tendencies until she admitted to the authorities her part in the crime. Although she faced certain imprisonment, she said she had more peace than ever before.

What this woman discovered is called "integrity." Many people limit the word to mean "honesty," but a more accurate definition is to be the same, inside and out.

A friend of mine, whom I'll call Alicia, has struggled with integrity for years. She was raised in a crime-ridden part of town by parents who were drinkers and carousers. When she was a teenager a church bus came to her neighborhood and took her to a ministry service, where she committed her life to Jesus Christ. But giving Him her *whole* life became a lifelong struggle. It was distressing for her to admit the way she was raised and the effects it had on her. She found it difficult to be honest, even with God.

Sometimes, like Alicia, we try to hide things from others. And we can become so skilled we attempt to do the same with God. Covering up only creates frustration. To some degree, it causes us to live a double life. There's no happy ending to Alicia's story, just a caution for all of us.

When I read the newspaper account of the woman who came clean and confessed her part in the robbery after all those years, I thought about the high price we pay when we don't have integrity. How easy life is when we are the same inside and out! Becoming honest with ourselves and with God may be painful at first, but the result is a deep, lasting peace—and a short time of pain is a small price to pay for the precious commodity of peace that is a result of a life of integrity.

MEDITATIONS:

"He who walks in integrity, who does what is right, and who speaks the truth in his heart...shall never be moved." Psalm 15:2,5 MLB

"Let integrity and uprightness preserve me; for I wait on thee." Psalm 25:21

ACTION STEPS:

To gain integrity, you'll have to start in private. Search your own heart first. Then allow God to purge you of all the pretenses and cover-ups you've developed.

Seek integrity. Pray for it as part of your daily prayers for yourself. King David, writer of the Psalms, had great integrity. Read through Psalms, one chapter each night, and let David's life encourage you.

The next time you find yourself not telling the complete truth—misrepresenting yourself as you really are or out-and-out lying—remove yourself from the situation for a "time out;" then get in touch with your private self once again. No one attending a party or a business lunch will miss you if you excuse yourself to powder your nose or step outside for a breath of fresh air. You'll leave that situation a happier, more peaceful person knowing you maintained your integrity.

THEY SHOULD KNOW:

"When a woman tells the truth she is creating the possibility for more truth around her."

Adrienne Rich
Poet and Writer

"Let the world know you as you are, not as you think you should be, because sooner or later, if you are posing, you will forget the pose, and then where are you?"

Fanny Brice
Singer, Actress

"It is worse than folly...not to recognize the truth, for in it lies the tinder for tomorrow."

Pearl S. Buck
Author

THINK ABOUT IT:

"He who walks in integrity walks securely, but he who perverts his ways will be found out." Proverbs 10:9 RSV

Work Ethic:

"Grandma, what does 'work ethic' mean?" my twelve-year-old granddaughter asked while working on her homework.

"Well, did you make your bed this morning?"

"Yes."

"Did you do the dishes tonight like your mother asked?"

"Yes."

"Then you understand the importance of work, which is the work ethic."

She thought for a while, then said, "Well, I didn't want to do it, so maybe I don't have a work ethic."

I wanted to laugh, but instead I seized the opportunity to influence her in a positive way. "It might still be taking hold in your life," I answered. "Once it does, you'll want to experience a job well done more than the fleeting rewards of laziness."

When I was twelve, I'm sure I didn't have a work ethic either. But maturity teaches us that a job well done is its own reward. When we give our lives to God, the value of a positive work ethic deepens even more. Every breath we take is a breath

God has given us in order to glorify Him. How much more is every job an opportunity to make Him proud of us.

Often people think glorifying God is limited to attending church services, singing in the choir or teaching Sunday school. But we actually glorify Him by working wholeheartedly at whatever we do. When we throw ourselves into our work, giving the task our all and best with every breath, striving for excellence, all of heaven takes note. And when we keep in mind all day how much He loves us and blesses us, it's easy to desire to do our best for Him.

MEDITATIONS:

"The fruit of the [uncompromisingly] righteous is a tree of life and he who is wise captures human lives *for God* [as a fisher of men]—he gathers and receives them *for eternity*." Proverbs 11:30 AMP

"Whatsoever thy hand findeth to do, do it with all thy might." Ecclesiates 9:10

ACTION STEPS:

❧ Do you have that one chore you hate doing? Next time you attempt it, try praying before you work and commit it to God for His glory. Then sing while you work—sing praise choruses to Him (not the Top 10). It will make the job pleasant and the work will go smoothly!

❧ Whatever you are doing, if there's a need for help, use the young people! The value of a strong work ethic seems to be slowly fading from our society, and they expect more and more to be done for them. Remember, you can positively influence the young men and women in your life. Doing things for them is not always the best policy. If they want to help you, let them. They should have the opportunity to experience tired feet and a sore back—as well as the satisfaction of a job well done.

❧ Years ago at a ranch in Texas owned by one of Edwin's relatives, my very young children worked for hours shelling black-eyed peas. When their great aunt finally cooked this traditional Texas dish, they ate it and loved it, even though it was new to them. I believe they continue to love black-eyed peas as much for the back-breaking labor they experienced shelling them as for the flavor of the delicious dish. The things we work hardest for are those we treasure most. In sports, playing hard at the game is what makes the winning sweet. Remember, the effort is as much a part of the victory as the rewards.

WORKING IT OUT:

"To love what you do and feel that it matters—how could anything be more fun?"

Katherine Graham

"Laziness may appear attractive, but work gives satisfaction."

Anne Frank
Diarist, Jewish
Holocaust Victim

"To feel valued, to know, even if only once in a while, that you can do a job well is an absolutely marvelous feeling."

Barbara Walters
Television Reporter

"I don't know anything about luck. I've never banked on it, and I'm afraid of people who do. Luck to me is something else—hard work, and realizing what is opportunity and what isn't."

Lucille Ball

Actress, Comedian

Contentment:

J ulia and I sang in the choir together. She appeared to be an unpretentious, demurely dressed woman with a simple home in a modest neighborhood. So when she invited my husband and me to dinner, we were surprised and delighted to be served a delicious meal presented on fine linens with a beautiful table setting. We never imagined that she and her husband had such luxuries. The example they set for us of humble contentment has remained with me throughout my adult life—they didn't want more, nor were they motivated by pride, even though they obviously had the means.

"Godliness with contentment is great gain" (1 Timothy 6:6). This is a biblical injunction too few of us live by! We strive to get wealth, possessions, and better houses, even though having Christ in our lives has already satisfied our deepest longings. Our friend Sue gets a new car, so we want one. Our neighbor Joe gets his own plane, so we want a plane. The children next door get a swimming pool, so we want one for our children.

The Apostle Paul evidently came from a well educated and prosperous family. Yet as he walked with God he declared, "I am abased and I abound, but whatever position I find myself in, I am content" Philippians 4:11,12 (author's paraphrase).

My pastor once gave an example of a couple who, after visiting their new, wealthy neighbors, went home to commiserate with each other about all they lacked by comparison. "Their furniture goes back to Louis the Fourteenth," the husband said, awestruck. The wife answered, "Yes, and ours goes back to Sears on the fifteenth!"

Competing with those who have more than we have will make us miserable. Some of the most unhappy people in the world have been some of the richest—and the poorest because they never saw the good in what they had. Like Paul, we can be miserable or content in whatever situation we find ourselves. It depends on what we make of it.

Gaining by possessing, earning or achieving, pales in comparison to gaining by contentment.

MEDITATIONS:

"But as for me, my contentment is in knowing You." Psalm 17:15 (author's paraphrase)

"Godliness with contentment is great gain" 1 Timothy 6:6

"Not that I speak in respect of want: for I have learned, in whatsoever state I am, therewith to be content. I know both how to be abased, and I know how to abound: every where and in all things I am instructed both to be full and to be hungry, both to abound and to suffer need. I can do all things through Christ which strengtheneth me." Philippians 4:11-13

ACTION STEPS:

❧ It could be that any unhappiness you feel is in areas where you've compared yourself to others. Breaking this habit is a discipline, but the reward is great once mastered. My husband had to complete a questionnaire before he received a physical examination. One question asked, "What kind of person are you?" and gave four choices: (a) happy (b) moderately happy (c) unhappy (d) very unhappy. Even my husband, who forgets momentary defeats and always looks to future victories, had to stop and consider this question. How about you?

❧ What are you striving for today? Are you certain your desire will bring satisfaction once you have fulfilled your aspiration? What good does it do to obtain all that we want? If we are unable to enjoy something unless we have it for ourselves, we will be miserable. Think of the Olympic gold medalist who pulls up the second- and third-ranked competitors to stand with her on her pedestal. They'll miss the glory of their achievement if they resent her win and decline her offer. Or the woman whose friend becomes engaged, and receives a gemstone three times larger than her own. She'll miss celebrating this special moment with her friend if she is envious. Those who are discontent miss so much, while the content enjoy most everything.

❧ A wise man traveling from a distant city met a young woman traveling toward that city. "What are the people like there?" the young woman asked. "Well what were people like where you came from?" the wise man asked. "Oh, they were horrid, selfish, cruel people and I am happy to leave them." "Well, daughter," the wise man answered, "I'm afraid the people in that distant city are the same."

Miles later he passed another young woman going toward the same city. "What are the people like there?" the young woman stopped to ask him. "Well, what were people like where you are coming from?" the wise man asked. "Oh, they were wonderful people—generous, friendly, and I shall miss them." "Well, you won't miss them long," said the wise man, "for you will meet many more just like them in the city where you are going."

Which young woman do you relate to? Work on those attitudes today!

YOU DON'T SAY:

"I've never sought success in order to get fame and money; it's the talent and the passion that count in success."

Ingrid Bergman
Actress

*"The pedigree of honey
Does not concern the bee;
A clover, any time, to him
Is aristocracy."*

Emily Dickinson[2]
Poet

LET'S PRAY:

Father, I have allowed frustration and anxiety to hinder my ability to see Your plan. Please forgive me for striving and grumbling. Teach me how to have contentment without giving up and to see Your purpose in everything I do. In Jesus' name I pray. Amen.

Insomnia:

A wake. Lying quietly listening to the neighborhood. Teen drivers squealing around corners—must be near their midnight curfew. The neighbor's sprinklers turn on—that's 1:00 a.m. The newspaper strikes the driveway—4:00 a.m. The foot fleeing of the jogger—5:00 a.m. The cat wants in—6:00 a.m. Car door slams, engine starts—6:30 a.m.

Sleeplessness, often frustrating, does not have to be a curse. Many of the greatest advancements for mankind came when Descartes, Einstein, or Edison took a quiet hour simply to think. For me, some of the greatest revelations and times of waiting and meditating on the things of God come in the early morning hours.

I used to get annoyed when I'd listen to those neighborhood sounds, unable to fall asleep though my body was exhausted. Then I thought, *What if God is trying to speak to me during these times?* Now I lie still and pray. Often I silently sing hymns and choruses.

When I adopt the attitude that my life is in God's hands, my frustrations slip away. God can speak to me, or He can direct me to pray. What better time to get my full attention than when there are no distractions?

Does the loss of an hour's sleep seem important when you can talk to the living God, receive instruction or comfort from

Him, and pray for someone by His direction? What may appear to be a curse can become an opportunity for blessing when we surrender to God's care for us.

Focus on your Lord in those sleepless hours and make them productive and peaceful. It may be just what you need to put you to sleep!

MEDITATIONS:

"To the righteous He gives peaceful sleep." Psalm 127:2 (author's paraphrase)

"Come to Me, all you who labor and are heavy-laden and over-burdened, and I will cause you to rest — I will ease and relieve and refresh your souls." Matthew 11:28 AMP

ACTION STEPS:

❧ Worry is a substitute for prayer. Don't worry. Pray things through.

❧ Keep a pad and pencil next to your bed. Often sleeplessness lingers when we are trying to remember something we haven't written down. Write it down and sleep!

❧ Ignore the television. If you have trouble sleeping, you don't need to hear something that triggers your mind in a certain direction. If you need to unwind, read your Bible or a good Christian novel to relax.

❧ Watch what you eat. Heavy dinners, chocolate ice cream, coffee after noontime, too much food, or too little food can all make falling asleep difficult. Let moderation be your guide.

❧ If you suffer from sleeplessness, keep a prayer list handy. If you share a room, keep a flashlight on your nightstand. Your prayers during sleepless hours can accomplish much good.

❧ If insomnia is truly problematic, pray for healing! God is faithful—He will direct you to the right help if you turn your thoughts away from worry and surrender yourself to Him.

ALERT THINKING:

"What if in my waking hours a sound should ring through the silent halls of hearing? What if a ray of light should flash through the darkened chambers of my soul? What would happen, I ask many and many a time. Would the bow-and-string tension of life snap? Would the heart, overweighted with sudden joy, stop beating for very excess of happiness?"

> Helen Keller
> Author, Social Activist

"I keep the telephone of my mind open to peace, harmony, health, love and abundance. Then whenever doubt, anxiety, or fear try to call me, they keep getting a busy signal and soon they'll forget my number."

> Edith Armstrong

LET'S PRAY:

Father, in the name of Jesus, I entrust my time of sleep to You. I set aside my cares and concerns. I ask for Your peace and surrender my will to Your purpose. Thank You for Your promise. You give Your beloved sleep. Amen.

Weaving Relationships

Relationships

Old Friends

"**T**all ones in back!" called the photographer. This group of dignified women suddenly became all elbows and legs, struggling to find our places. I headed for the back row where Mary was already positioned.

"Come on up, Nancy," she said.

"We know where we belong, don't we?" I answered as I grabbed her hand to step to the top tier of the riser. "Do you remember when you grew four inches between your freshman and sophomore years?"

"Oh, Nancy! My own mother doesn't even remember that!" Mary exclaimed. "And my children have never believed I grew that fast. I'm so glad someone remembers!"

The day was full of old acquaintances and memories. The years had brought their changes. We stood again where we once stood, wearing navy blue uniforms, but now wearing years of experience brought by marriage, children and careers. Yet we discovered the long gaps between Christmas cards and past conversations had not prevented the rekindling of our relationships, for the embers were still aglow.

There is a sense of incomparable joy remembering a shared adventure together. Nothing can replace the particular feeling of belonging you experience when you renew old friendships.

True friendships are like warm, slow-burning logs. They are voluntary, chosen investments. Renewing a forgotten friendship is like receiving a dividend from a prior deposit. When you redeem it there is a sense of continuity and stability that makes you rich.

MEDITATIONS:

Read about David and Jonathan's friendship. 1 Samuel 18:1-4

"A friend loves at all times." Proverbs 17:17 RSV

ACTION STEPS:

❧ Choose any period of your life and look back, remembering only the positives. "Going back" is impossible because former days are gone; however, people and memories remain. Their sweetness is for us to savor.

❧ The next time you have the opportunity, go to a reunion or place where you'll meet people from another period of your life. People remember things about us that are jewels to discover. Their perspective may be far different from ours, especially if our memories are negative. We're generally critical of ourselves in remembering our actions and immaturity. Others are far more generous.

❧ Every friendship in which we invest ourselves enriches our lives. Make a goal of making a new friend this week, this month, or this year.

POETS KNOW IT:

"My candle burns at both ends;
It will not last the night;
But ah, my foes, and oh, my friends—
It gives a lovely light.
"A Few Figs"

Edna St. Vincent Millay[3]
Poet

"I smile to think that days remain
Perhaps to me in which, though bread be sweet
No more, and red wine warm my blood in vain,
I shall be glad remembering how the fleet,
Lithe poppies ran like torchmen with the wheat."

Helen Jackson[4]
Writer

Friends:

The same year Malcolm Forbes threw his million-dollar birthday bash, I attended a party Linda's friend threw for her. From reports I read about Malcolm's, I believe Linda's outshone his.

Most of Linda's friends were busy people who could easily have declined the invitation. Yet they responded from across the nation. They came in person, sent telegrams, flowers, cards and gifts. None of her acquaintances came because of business ties, for Linda knew them outside of work. None came because they were family, for Linda had little family. None came because of Linda's wealth, for apart from friendships, she had few riches. Instead, her guests came to celebrate their love for Linda and hers for them.

I thought about that party for a long while afterward. It caused me to reflect on all the friends I've had through the years and how few with whom I still keep in touch. Many of us exchange notes with our Christmas cards, but beyond that, we don't really communicate. Such friendships can easily die for lack of nurturing.

Linda is positively rich in true friendships because she has nurtured them. She offers an open door, an attentive ear on the telephone, and generosity with her time. People sense her unselfish, genuine spirit and flock to her.

The world is hungry for true friends—people who are not around out of convenience or self-seeking. When we offer true friendship, generously giving whatever we have available, we can increase our friendships and become richer than a billionaire!

MEDITATION:

"A man that hath friends must shew himself friendly." Proverbs 18:24

ACTION STEPS:

&❧ We can reestablish relationships simply by getting in touch with former friends—through class reunions, looking others up when we pass through their city, or just calling on the telephone. List three people you want to communicate with; one by phone, one by mail and one in person. Make a plan to do it this month.

&❧ Sometimes we find things in gift shops that remind us of a certain person. Perhaps one old friend collects thimbles, another cats, mice or cows. If it's not too large or expensive why not send it to the one you are thinking of? Amusing gifts cheer the soul. Serious gifts warm the heart. Either way, your friend will be happy at your thoughtfulness, realizing you still care.

&❧ Start every conversation with your friends for the next two weeks with something nice about them. Compliment them on their looks, minds or hearts. Remind them of something they once did for you that helped you. Or just tell them frankly how much you appreciate their friendship!

GREAT MINDS THINK ALIKE:

"Nobody sees a flower—really—it is so small—we haven't time— and to see takes time like to have a friend takes time."

Georgia O'Keefe

Artist

"Loneliness is the most terrible poverty."

Mother Teresa

LET'S PRAY:

Dear Father, help me to be a friend. You've been so good to me; You've been my friend and counselor. By Your Spirit, direct me to those who need encouragement and Your love. In Jesus' name. Amen.

Peacemakers:

The first rays of sunshine on a peaceful spring morning felt glorious on Joan's face as she stepped onto her back porch to drink her early morning coffee. Suddenly, a shout broke through her reverie.

"Turn out that light at night! It shines in my bedroom and I can't sleep!" an angry woman yelled from beyond the fence.

Shocked, Joan still managed to respond politely. She lived alone in this growing neighborhood, and the back porch light was a security measure. She called me and several other friends quite distraught. She then decided to attempt a gesture of peace and replaced her porch light with a dimmer bulb.

The next day the neighbor again yelled at her. For a second time, Joan overcame her anger. That night she directed the light to shine away from the neighbor's home. A few mornings later she stepped outside to discover her light fixture laying in pieces on the concrete patio. Her friends suggested calling the police. Joan said, "Not yet," and replaced the light.

Then the irate neighbor telephoned Joan, screaming, "Turn out that light or I'll go to the Homeowners Association!"

Now Joan was deeply upset. This woman maintained tremendous influence with the other homeowners. Joan called me in tears and together we prayed. She was still hesitant to start any action herself.

On the night of the homeowners' meeting, the committee dismissed the neighbor's complaint as if she was without any influence and quickly moved to other business. It seemed to be miraculous. Joan saw God answering our prayer. Weeks later while taking a walk, she crossed paths with the surly woman. "Hello neighbor!" Joan said, with a huge smile. The sputtering neighbor's hesitation allowed Joan to launch into a brief conversation. Days later the same scenario was repeated.

Still, Joan wondered if the situation was completely over. But months later, while walking in a shopping mall, she heard quickening footsteps behind her and felt two arms enclose her in a huge bear hug. Joan spun around as quickly as she could untangle herself, and looked directly into the laughing eyes of her former enemy and neighbor!

Joan had the choice to feud or be a peacemaker, to be a foe or become a friend. She made the right choice. Her light shone both outside her home and inside her heart. Keeping her peace, she chose the way of peace, and received peace as her reward.

There's hardly anything in life more valuable than peace. Jesus said we're blessed and are God's sons (daughters) meaning His heirs, if we make peace. We must first make peace inside ourselves, then spread it to others. The Bible says Jesus "kept His peace." And that same peace, Jesus said, "I give (bequeath) to you" (See John 14:27). That means we can walk in the unhurried, unworried peace that Jesus had because we are God's heirs.

MEDITATIONS:

"Blessed are the peacemakers: for they shall be called the children of God." Matthew 5:9

"Shall not God avenge his own elect, which cry day and night unto him...he will avenge them speedily." Luke 18:7,8

"Vengeance belongeth unto me, I will recompense, saith the Lord." Hebrews 10:30

"Let your light so shine before men, that they may see your good works, and glorify your Father which is in heaven." Matthew 5:16

ACTION STEPS:

❧ Make a list of everything that disturbs your peace. List the things in the last day, week or month that have upset you. See if there's a pattern. If Satan can, he'll steal your peace, but he'll attempt to do it the same way every time. Pray over your list, item by item. When you encounter those situations again, resist the devil, and submit them to God before you have a chance to lose your peace over them.

❧ Sometimes the most obvious response to situations is the last one we think of. The Bible says to pray for our enemies and to delight when men despitefully use us. List some "enemies" or people who have misused you and spend some time in prayer over them. Does God want you to get away from them? To confront them? To forgive them?

❧ Women who fend for themselves often fight first, then pray later. Joan's remarkable restraint turned a difficult situation that could have begun years of feuding into an opportunity for a relationship. Are there opportunities for good that you've misread as obstacles to fight? The Lord will guide you in the right direction when you step back long enough to prayerfully submit them to Him.

SO TRUE:

"Courage is the price that life exacts for granting peace."
Amelia Earhart
Aviatrix

"People who fight fire with fire usually end up with ashes."
Abigail Van Buren
Advice Columnist

$\mathscr{L}$istening:

Brimming with news, I called an old friend, certain she would be thrilled to hear what I had to say. "Hello, Brenda!" I said when her cheery voice answered the telephone.

"Nancy? I can't believe it! How are you?"

"I'm fine, how are you?" That was as far as I got.

Brenda told me about her health, husband, children, house and career. For a long time I listened, waiting for her to catch her breath so I could interject the reason I called. Instead, she only paused a moment for me to make a polite comment of agreement, approval or assent. Still I remained hopeful. Any minute, I thought, she'll stop and then I'll tell her the news.

At last she finished, but only to say she had to go somewhere, so we hung up. Deflated, frustrated and flat, I mused about not being able to share my news. Humbled by the experience, I thought, "One day I'll tell her and she won't remember this conversation at all. She'll just say, 'Well, why didn't you stop me?'"

As I returned the telephone to its cradle, I remembered the times I'd been on the other end—doing all the talking while someone else listened. How embarrassing to be caught being self-centered! People have often said that listening is an art. I believe it is. Think of the things people try to tell us every day that we miss. Not only good news, but important things, a child's question, or worries we could dispel and lift from our mother's mind, or words of wisdom from an acquaintance that would redirect our course.

How often are we too busy, too full of thoughts and plans, to hear the softly spoken words to our hearts that God wants us to hear? Cutting someone off with mindless chatter is more than just bad manners. We can miss our chance to achieve our purpose in life just by being so busy in our minds and with our mouths that we don't hear the Holy Spirit. He can speak directly to our hearts or through the mouth of someone else.

MEDITATION:

"Wherefore, my beloved brethren, let every man be swift to hear, slow to speak, slow to wrath." James 1:19

ACTIONS STEPS:

❧ Listen to your children. The times they appear withdrawn or pensive require extra sensitivity on your part, whether they are small or grown. If they are young, something at school may have disturbed them. Adult children may experience difficulty discussing marriage or childrearing problems. You will miss your opportunity to share your insight with them if you're too busy to hear with your heart. Listen to teenagers especially. Everyone around them at that age is vying for attention. They need you to be listening, loving, and supportive.

❧ Take one day just to listen to others. Or, try only to listen to a friend who is quiet, or to one who talks quite a bit. They may be saying more than you've ever guessed if you stop long enough to hear.

LISTEN TO HER:

"I like people who refuse to speak until they are ready to speak."
Lillian Hellman
Writer

LET'S PRAY:

Father, I come to You in Jesus' name to ask You to help me to have listening ears and a hearing heart. Don't let me miss those opportunities You direct into my life, to encourage, praise and console a friend, a family member, a neighbor or a stranger. Thank You for Your patience. Amen.

THINK ABOUT IT:

"Talking is sharing, but listening is caring."
Jeannie Caldwell
Christian Author

Friendships:

Loyalty can be a wonderful trait, yet as we see in gangs and cults, it can sometimes prove deadly. In friendships, loyalty can be deadly in another way.

Friends of mine, Sharon and Becky, seemed entirely compatible when they met. They enjoyed the same things, shared similar ideas and encouraged each other to achieve positive goals. Their relationship blossomed. But after a few months, Becky began to fear the vulnerability and intimacy of true friendship. She withdrew from Sharon, and quickly invested her interest in another friend with whom she and Sharon were acquainted.

This left Sharon feeling betrayed, bewildered, confused and hurt. When Sharon came to me for counsel, I reflected on my own friendships. Out of hundreds of friends I've made through the years, those with whom I still maintain a close, active relationship, is a startlingly small number. The others may still be on my Christmas card list, but some of them I haven't seen in years.

I told Sharon that Becky may well come around and be sorry for the hurt she caused her. But I warned Sharon to go on and make new friends, and not become like Becky, afraid to invest in true friendship.

Keeping some friends is more detrimental than profitable. Friends who use us, influence us to do negative things, or bring us down are not good friends to keep. Many people struggle with letting go of negative friendships, because they're concerned they're being disloyal. But loyalty in that case is a vice more than a virtue.

Our friendships change naturally as our lives progress. Loyalty to others does not exclude loyalty to ourselves. The loss of intimacy in some friendships does not for one minute spoil the richness of true friendship.

MEDITATION:

"Those who devise good meet loyalty and faithfulness." Proverbs 14:22 RSV

ACTION STEPS:

❧ Are you friends with someone who almost always leaves you feeling down? Or whom you are always having to cheer up? Perhaps it is time to gently ease away, decrease your intimacy, and seek out a new friend who encourages you. This is not disloyal. It is wise.

❧ Generally friends have the same interests or share something in common that brings them together. If one grows beyond the other in socio-economic status, education or emotion, the friendship can wither and ultimately die. When the two become equal again in years to come, the two may resume as if nothing ever happened. These ebbs and tides in life are normal, not to be feared, and will work out for us as we keep them before the Lord in prayer and continue to follow Him.

❧ Our loyalty is rightfully called into question when we become friends with people for a specific purpose. If we're nice to the loan officer at the bank only when we need to fix up the house, we're not true friends with her! Learn to correctly discern between friendship and using others, then practice loyalty with your true friends.

FRIENDLY CHATTER:

"Love is like the wild rose briar;
Friendship like the holly tree.
The holly is dear when the rose briar blooms,
But which will bloom more constantly?"

Emily Jane Bronte[5]
Writer

"*It is wise to apply the oil of refined politeness to the mechanism of friendship.*"

Colette
Writer

Life and Death:

HIGH SCHOOL REUNION

The sun shone brightly as my sister Ellen and I stepped onto her leaf-strewn front porch. We breathed in cool, damp air that was tinged with the autumn scents of recent rain on golden leaves. The day seemed intent on welcoming me home for a visit with my sisters in Brookline, and was perfect for our high school reunion at Mount Saint Joseph Academy.

As we walked to the car, I thought about my former classmates. Many of them came from good neighborhoods that begat the Kennedys, Longfellows, Lowells and Adams. Others had parents who struggled to fulfill their belief in private education. Many girls I remembered were naturally great achievers. For weeks I had anticipated this reunion and wondered what the passing of time had brought each of us. Finally arriving, I drew open the heavy old wooden schoolhouse door with apprehension.

"Now who is this?" queried the first woman I saw. "Oh, of course—Nancy! How good to see you."

In a flash I was hugged and handed around to the nineteen attending from my class. Ellen's class and others balanced out the lively group. Conversations flowed and ebbed as I talked with the women from my class. It was interesting to see the different occupations they had chosen. Some coordinated child raising with a career, others had very large families. Most all of them were energetic doers—whether at home, church or work.

As friendships rekindled, I recognized that the passing of time was an equalizer. Where once my friendships revolved around earned grades equivalent to mine, now I felt aligned with those who lived lives similar to mine. Janet with her eight children seemed more of a peer now than when she was a straight-A student. (I wasn't!) Where once the class was separated by economics, geography and talent, today we were united by maturity, shared history, and a perception of the world formed during those early years of burgeoning adulthood.

But time equalizes in a different way also. I was saddened to learn that thirteen of our graduating class would not attend another reunion on this side of heaven. When time runs out it brings us the greatest common denominator of all: eternity.

I walked down the steps toward the car and looked back. *Who will be at the next reunion,* I wondered, *and who will be missing?* I thanked God my faith hadn't stopped at the steps of Mount Saint Joseph's. I prayed that my classmates would all know Christ's love and make Him their Lord. Eternity will be so much the sweeter when the reunion never ceases.

MEDITATIONS:

"To all who received him, he gave the right to become children of God. All they needed to do was to trust him to save them." John 1:12 TLB

"If we confess our sins to him, he can be depended on to forgive us and to cleanse us from every wrong. [And it is perfectly proper for God to do this for us because Christ died to wash away our sins.]" 1 John 1:9 TLB

Jesus said, "I go and prepare a place for you...that where I am, there ye may be also." John 14:2,3

ACTION STEPS:

❧ Many people fail to achieve their goals in life because of lack of planning. But preparing for the afterlife is the most important plan anyone will ever make. Consider today where you will be tomorrow. Accept the provision of Jesus Christ to become a child of God. Make yourself welcome in heaven by admitting you are not able to get there on your own, but need Christ's forgiveness and love in order to be welcomed with open arms to the greatest reunion ever.

PRAY THIS PRAYER:

God, I accept responsibility for my life, for everything I've done and said. I apologize to You for the wrong things I've done and the times I've lived as though You didn't exist. Please forgive me. I accept the fact that Jesus Christ died then rose from the dead to break the power of sin and death off of those who believe in Him. I admit that He is your Son, that He is alive today, and that believing in Him is the only way You will allow me to become Your child. Today I give up the way I've been living and surrender myself completely to You, trusting You to guide me through the rest of my life and into eternity. In Jesus' name I pray. Amen.

❧ Ensure that your friends and relatives will join you in heaven by praying for them and, if they are willing, with them. You can make all the difference—an eternal difference—by praying for them.

LOVE NOTE:

"Love is the only thing that we can carry with us when we go, and it makes the end so easy."

Louisa May Alcott
Writer

Tied in Knots

THREE

Crisis:

OPPORTUNITY!

"I could hire two younger guys for the salary I'm paying Darin," the new, young CEO reasoned, and suddenly fifty-six-year-old Darin was looking for work. In another state, Bruce, for years the top salesman in his firm, watched his commissions climb until the company decided it could no longer afford him. At age fifty-five he was ignominiously fired.

Both Darin's and Bruce's wives were shocked and panicked. They had expected their well-paid husbands to continue with the company, collect a fat retirement, and provide for them in the manner to which they were accustomed 'til death did them part.

Instead, they were forced to return to the meager uncertainty they had lived through in their twenties. Back then, the hopes of building, dreaming, and planning had given them joy. But the joys of attaining had long since dissolved into the routine of maintaining.

Often in our upward mobility we don't realize the pressures that close in on us from our choice of lifestyle. As we gain the freedom of having money, we lose the freedom of a carefree attitude toward possessions and property. Losing your livelihood, though tragic, can be an opportunity to recover a different kind of freedom, and a different kind of joy, if you'll look at your circumstance in a new way.

When Darin and his wife were forced to sell their home, she took some of the money and went overseas to visit a relative—something she had wanted to do for years but didn't think they could afford! Bruce's wife redirected her efforts into an inexpensive hobby. She became such an expert that she was hired by a local firm and emerged from her crisis as a career woman.

Though the crisis is real, the fact that it does not end our lives is equally real. With God using our ingenuity and creativity, we can rediscover the joys that success threatened to suppress.

ACTION STEPS:

❧ Give yourself your own wake-up call if you are complacent or stagnant. None of us want a big jolt to wake us. Review your options. Many people in frightening circumstances react negatively without considering positive options. Although both Darin and Bruce filed age discrimination lawsuits, neither collected. Courts are fickle, so don't trust in them.

❧ Make a list of your desires. What have you always wanted to do? Perhaps writing, painting or acting in the fine arts. Starting your own business, opening a specialty store, or working up through corporate ranks in the business realm could be your unfulfilled dream. You may have wanted to be a travel agent, an animal trainer, or a dock supervisor in the trades and services. Be completely honest.

Now, list your strengths. What do you do well? If you have served as a wife and mother without outside work, you are well-trained in cashiering, being a personal shopper, coaching, cooking, sales, hospital aid, administrator, financial wizard, all-round "girl Friday" or any work involving the support of another person or group of people.

Generally, we have to make a living doing what we already do well, not necessarily what we want to do. By putting your hand to the plow in a realistic, focused effort you will ride out your crisis. Then, holding the vision of your real dreams, work toward them, even if you have to do it after hours, until eventually you can make a living doing what you really wanted to do all along. People reach their goals by going forward a step at a time, focusing on the end result, yet keeping a level head right where they are.

M E D I T A T I O N :

"You will keep on guiding me all my life with your wisdom and counsel; and afterwards receive me into the glories of heaven!" Psalm 73:24 TLB

E X P E R I E N C E   S P E A K S :

"When life gives you lemons, make lemonade."
> Erma Bombeck
> Humorist, Writer

"You don't seem to realize that a poor person who is unhappy is in a better position than a rich person who is unhappy. Because the poor person has hope. He thinks money would help."
> Jean Kerr
> Writer

Sickness:

I always looked forward to the fun of each birthday until two years ago when the candle count seemed to match the number of aches and pains I had. While traveling through an icy climate in another country, pneumonia found its path to me. When I got home to recover, I discovered a serious infection on the bottom of my foot. Then flu attacked.

After years of raising children and grandchildren, keeping house, looking after my husband—even shopping for his clothes—my husband and family were now waiting on me hand and foot. To my surprise, I enjoyed the attention. And staying in bed seemed a formerly forbidden luxury—for a while. I soon became bored, then concerned as I thought about people I had known who took to their beds, never to get up again. The romance quickly faded and I knew it was time for action.

The next day I struggled to get up, only to hobble on our hard tile floors with a painfully sore foot, dizzy at every step. I forced myself again the second day, then the third, but at least I was up!

One day as I tottered weakly over my plastic tub, routinely soaking my foot, the Lord spoke to my heart and showed me I had accepted defeat. It hadn't occurred to me that I had given in or given up. With my foot still soaking, I repented and added a stepped-up prayer campaign to my action plan. I placed myself in the hands of the Lord and prayed aloud, rebuking the powers of Satan that tried to pull me down, declaring myself a servant of the living God and quoting scriptures on healing from the Bible. Some dear friends sent me another scripture that bolstered me. After several days, spiritual strength overcame bodily weakness and at last my body began to heal.

What a mistake to believe that because we are getting older, we should accept defeat—that we should grow weaker, more fearful, going under instead of staying on top. How strong we can become when God's Spirit through our spirit rules our lives.

HEALING SCRIPTURES:

Deuteronomy 7:15

Psalm 41:3,4

Psalm 103:2-5

Psalm 107:19,20—"Then they cry unto the Lord in their trouble, and he saveth them out of their distresses. He sent his word, and healed them, and delivered them from their destructions."

Isaiah 53:4,5 RSV—"Surely he has borne our griefs and carried our sorrows; yet we esteemed him stricken, smitten by God, and afflicted. But he was wounded for our transgressions, he was bruised for our iniquities; upon him was the chastisement that made us whole, and with his stripes we are healed.

Jeremiah 17:14

Matthew 14:36

Mark 2:11,12

Luke 4:18

Acts 5:16

James 5:14-16

1 Peter 2:24 RSV—"He himself bore our sins in his body on the tree, that we might die to sin and live to righteousness. By his wounds you have been healed."

3 John 2

ACTION STEPS:

❧ If you are in a predicament with illness, don't give up! God is always there to heal, comfort, fill your life with joy, and He will enable you to overcome every tempting thought of quitting.

❧ Make a list of things you enjoy doing, and keep doing them. When you feel like giving up to disability, review your list and fight that fight!

❧ Find someone to pray with you on a regular basis, a strong, mature Christian who will challenge you when you start to give up.

❧ Memorize this verse and repeat it every morning as you work out the kinks when you first wake up: Many are the afflictions of the righteous but the Lord delivers (insert your name here) out of them all. (See Psalm 34:19)

❧ Exercise your faith by quoting scripture. Any of the previous verses are good, as is: James 4:7,8 "Submit yourselves therefore to God. Resist the devil, and he will flee from you. Draw nigh to God, and he will draw nigh to you."

WORTH QUOTING:

"I believe one thing: that today is yesterday and tomorrow is today and you can't stop. Sensitivity is not made dull by age."
> Martha Graham
> Dancer

"I gain strength, courage and confidence by every experience in which I must stop and look fear in the face...I say to myself, I've lived through this and can take the next thing that comes along...we must do the things we think we cannot do."
> Eleanor Roosevelt
> Writer,
> Humanitarian,
> U. N. Delegate,
> First Lady

LET'S PRAY:

Father, I receive Your blessing of health. Your promise to take sickness from the midst of us shows me Your will, and I believe by Jesus' stripes I am whole and delivered from infirmities. In Jesus' name I pray. Amen.

Moving:

MIND OVER MATTER

A family from the northern United States moved down the street from our southern California home complete with sleds and snow shovels, to the amusement of the neighborhood. We all had a good laugh some years later when they finally conceded and gave away the shovels.

In the U.S. today, most people frequently move. At any age, we can find it traumatic. We can approach it with wide-eyed amazement wondering, "How did I ever accumulate so much stuff?"

On the up side, moving provides the opportunity to pull out things we don't want, didn't need after all, or will find unnecessary in our new home. Then there is the downside. First, the nerves over whether our carefully packed items will survive or even fit the new home. Secondly, we face the adjustment to a new church, new community, new friends, new schools, and sometimes new foods, customs and culture.

When I left California, I wanted to put to good use all the things I didn't need, so I sent a pair of almost new turquoise shoes to my niece in New York who shares my shoe size. She sent a humorous letter back saying thank you but that she was a Yankee and where she lived women wore mostly brown or black. I'd been away from the East so long I'd forgotten how conservative it was.

Every region has distinct customs and a culture all its own. We can create more trauma if we insist on doing things the way we did them "back home." We can bore new friends if we only wish to talk about how things were "back on the ranch." We need to stay open to learn what they love about the place we now share, where to eat and shop, where to worship, and the hidden treasures that only inquisitive minds can find.

We make adjustments for the change of seasons each year without distress. If only we would adapt to new turns in our lives as easily as we respond to the next seasons, we could discover that each new experience has joys of its own. To keep your eyes on what is past is to miss the joys of where you are.

Find what suits your personality and adapt it to your new home. Send those turquoise shoes West, and the snow shovels North!

MEDITATION:

"The Lord's curse is on the house of the wicked, but he blesses the abode of the righteous." Proverbs 3:33 RSV

ACTION STEPS:

❧ Pay attention to people who are proud of where they live. Find out what makes them love "home." If you've just moved to their area, share some of their experiences until you begin to appreciate it too.

❧ If you are older, when it's time to move—MOVE! Don't put your children through the agony of wondering how you are doing all alone at the old house. If they encourage you to move to smaller quarters, to their home or to a retirement center, take those suggestions seriously. Don't look only at the sorrow of what you'll miss. Look at the joys of discovering new things and making new friends. Accept the changing seasons of your life. But don't be too quick to move either. Give it lots of prayer and deliberate planning.

❧ Stay in touch with old friends, but not at the expense of making new ones. With as much as you love your old friends, there's no way of knowing if your best friend is yet to be found.

GOOD POINT:

"When one door of happiness closes, another opens; but often we look so long at the closed door that we do not see the one which has been opened for us."

> Helen Keller
> Author, Social
> Activist

"Nothing in life is to be feared. It is only to be understood."

> Marie Curie
> Physician, Scientist

Lost:

When we moved to Texas a couple of years ago, it took me awhile to remember where things were in my new house. It took even longer to figure out where I was on the roadways! Even though I had lived in southern California with all its freeways, it seems like there were more freeways in Dallas, which can be intimidating.

One day I found my way to a huge shopping center miles away from my home. But on the way back home, I just kept driving. Nothing looked right. "Have I missed a turn?" I thought. Then I saw the city of Dallas off to my left and realized it shouldn't be there. One of us was in the wrong place!

"Lord, help me," I whispered. I finally stopped and asked directions. When I arrived home much later, my husband suggested that maybe they took down the signs due to construction. It sounded good, I readily agreed, but to my chagrin, the next time I came home from the mall the signs were clearly there.

The Lord helps me with directions continually. Usually it's directions for my life that He gives me. But He also helps me with physical things such as guiding my car. I can just whisper His name, and rely on Him to get me home.

When we don't know where we're going, we must rely on the Lord and trust Him, not ourselves. Unlike us, He is always right and He'll never steer us wrong.

MEDITATION:

"I am the Lord your God, who teaches you to profit, who leads you in the way you should go." Isaiah 48:17 RSV

ACTION STEPS:

❧ How many times each day do you ask God for direction? Have you become so self-contented that you don't think you need to ask anymore? It might be time to check with Him, asking if He has a new direction He wants you to go in.

❧ There is power in the name of Jesus. When you have a difficult situation, crisis, or moment of truth, just calling out His name releases the power of heaven to help you. Say it often, and say it without hesitation: Jesus!

❧ A good map is a valuable tool! Whether you've been in your city for a year or ten years, put a good map in your car today so you'll have it when that unexpected crisis arises.

SHE SAID:

"Trust the Lord and He will bring you across the finish line."
Joyce Meyer
Christian Author

FUN STUFF:

"The suburbs were discovered, quite by accident, one day in the early 1940's by a Welcome Wagon lady who was lost."
Erma Bombeck
Humorist, Writer

Crisis:

I t's odd to realize a crisis can become a cherished memory. We hear people say things like, "Remember how the neighbors pitched in to help during the hurricane?"

I recall a young couple in our church whose first baby lived only a few hours after its birth — an immense tragedy of trauma and heartbreak! But for the first time other church members became aware of this quiet, reserved couple who had worshipped with us for many months. Our hearts and hands were extended to embrace them with God's love and compassion.

During their calamity the love that surrounded them became a precious demonstration of the grace of our mighty God. Later they were able to have other children. Our church members as well as this couple became stronger Christians as God brought us together through their tragedy and into a shared joy.

Crisis will strengthen our faith if we use it for this purpose.

Our first pastorate was in a small mountain community in northern California. The board of elders put us on a percentage basis for our income, based on how much came in each week through tithes and offerings. It sounded fair. In June when we began to pastor the church, the income was adequate. But because many of the men worked in the lumber industry and their slow time came during the winter, then our income took a nose-dive. What a shock!

We had financed a car in the summer, but couldn't make the payments by winter. So we turned it in on an old wreck that wheezed and gasped as if it were dying—and it finally did. But I still have a touch of nostalgia when I think of that old heap. What a crisis! But by remembering it, I remember how God brought us through.

When crisis comes, we think we will never live through it— but we do. God in His infinite creativity gets us through, often in ways we would never have imagined. As we come through the crisis our faith in God is stronger, for our faith actually increases, our knowledge of the ways of God deepens and we may even find friends we never knew we had.

MEDITATIONS:

"Don't worry...I have overcome the world." John 16:33 (author's paraphrase)

"My peace I give to you, not as the world gives." John 14:27 (author's paraphrase)

ACTION STEPS:

&. If you are in crisis, pray for God to act creatively. Although you may think of a hundred solutions, give God permission to work in His way. Release it to Him and continue to pray until you know God has it in hand and is working it out.

&. When Jesus went through the crisis of the Cross, He kept His peace. In the same way, when we are in crisis, we need to keep our peace. Your mind will fight against that, as you think of every way you can be saved. Turn off your mind. Feed God's Word to your spirit. Rest in God and His help. Victory will eventually come as you read your Bible, pray and walk in obedience to Him.

THEY SAID IT:

"Trouble is a part of life, and if you don't share it, you don't give the person who loves you a chance to love you enough."
Dinah Shore
Singer, Actress

"We are not interested in the possibilities of defeat."
Queen Victoria of England

"Any person who chooses God's way to handle his problems and hurtful situations is destined for great things."
Joyce Meyer
Christian Author

LET'S PRAY:

Father, I look to Your creativity and rest in Your love as You work all things to Your good. In Jesus' name. Amen.

Fear:

Edwin and I pioneered a church and although we were pastoring, we were barely three years old in the Lord. We had much to learn! We lived in a tiny three-room parsonage attached to the church building. Neither of us will ever forget the fright we had while we lived there.

Late one Saturday night as I was in the bathroom preparing for Sunday, I heard the back door latch move. I called out in a loud whisper to my sleeping husband, "Edwin, there's something at the back door!"

He stumbled out of bed, I heard his footsteps in the kitchen, and movement in the back of the house. Then came his anguished cry. "MY LORD, PAUL HAS BEEN KIDNAPPED!"

The back door stood open, and Paul's bed in the children's room was empty. The nation had lived through the Lindbergh baby kidnapping some time before and with those images in our minds, we panicked.

I screamed and joined Edwin who was on the telephone to the police. We waited in shock, checking and rechecking each room and crying, "Jesus, Jesus." Suddenly our little blonde sleepy-eyed Paul wandered through the back door and into the house.

Even though he was barely four years old, he understood the commotion and explained at once that since I was in the bathroom, he went outside to relieve himself.

In just minutes after our call the police were searching the backyard. Edwin tried to explain to them what happened. They were as distressed as we were, but they finally understood and left.

I will never forget the fear and anguish that gripped my heart in those few minutes when I thought I had lost my son. Fear triggers adrenalin to our bodies that can give us the surge of strength necessary to ride out the crisis. But a prolonged, constant state of fear is terribly unhealthy. Jesus admonished us to fear not.

Life can be filled with perplexities and real dangers but we can trust God that whatever the circumstances, He will bring us through. Trusting in Him is the antidote to the state of fear. Once past, we can sometimes even laugh about our reactions.

MEDITATION:

"The Lord is my helper, and I will not fear what man shall do unto me." Hebrews 13:6

ACTION STEPS:

❧ Fear is believing that something you cannot see will happen. Faith is believing that something you cannot see will happen. The difference is that fear is based on negative thinking and attracts negative results. Faith is based on positive thinking and attracts positive results. Replace fear with faith in God and start seeing some different results!

❧ In my first *Tapestry* book, I described the tiny parsonage we lived in when this incident happened, and another fearful incident when I thought we were being attacked by a bear while camping. Those are two of my favorite vignettes which always pick me up when I reread them. It might be just because it's my life! But if you have that book, you could try rereading them too.

THEY KNOW FEAR:

"The peace of God that passes all understanding is very real and more powerful than any pressure that fear can bring."

Linda Asbury
Christian Author

"A person who is filled with wisdom and love will think a matter through, seek and receive direction from the Lord, and handle the situation in a balanced way."

Joyce Meyer
Christian Author

LET'S PRAY:

Heavenly Father, I come into Your presence and receive Your protection and love, for there is no fear in love and I know according to Your Word You have not given me the spirit of fear, but of power, and of love, and of a sound mind. Thank You for Your peace. In Jesus' name. Amen.

"They might try robbery." "Jay may kill himself." "What if they hurt someone?" "My family is falling apart...."

As my friend Jane tried to fall asleep, such thoughts filled her mind, causing total disarray, like slides on a screen after the projector tray had spilled — void of order or reason, irrational and unrelated. Her teenagers had run away, and her husband, Jay, was distraught.

During previous rebellious episodes, Jay maintained a firm hold on God and had gently comforted his wife. But now that his children seemed bent on disobedience, he was completely broken. Nothing Jane said or did comforted him.

Jane struggled through both crises in seeming isolation. Her mind brimmed with foreboding, negative thoughts. She told me that each time she started to pray she would suddenly realize she wasn't praying anymore, but merely rehearsing the memories of the terrible climax of events.

Parenting is just one area of life in which crisis can produce extreme anxiety to the point of breakdown. Instead of trying to control the situation, we're better off surrendering our helplessness to God. On an everyday basis we tend to handle things with our own strength, not realizing that apart from God we cannot even draw our next breath. Through crisis, God teaches us to acknowledge and trust Him.

Jane told me later her mind prepared for the worst, convincing her that only bad would happen and she could not depend on God. Finally one night, she acknowledged that she could not influence her husband or children aside from prayer. Accepting utter helplessness, Jane surrendered herself to the loving Heavenly Father. When she did, sleep came immediately.

Surrender to Jesus Christ brings peace at the point of salvation, when we exchange our sins for His righteousness. As we grow, each new surrender brings us closer to our Savior, more trusting of our God, and more able to outlast any storm peacefully. Today, Jane's children have grown up, her husband is fine, and she is wiser and stronger than ever.

MEDITATIONS:

"Come to Me all you who labor and are heavily burdened, and I will give you rest." Matthew 11:28 MLB

"Be strong and courageous; have no fear, nor be at all in dread...for it is the Lord your God who is going with you; He will neither fail you nor forsake you." Deuteronomy 31:6 MLB

ACTION STEPS:

❧ Once we admit our helplessness in a situation, we must follow up with resolute prayer. People who feel helpless tend to give up instead of pressing on. We must press on, but in the power of God's Spirit, not ourselves. When I had a hopelessly wayward child, I started praying and God seemed to lead my prayers to specific areas of her life that, apart from Him, I had no knowledge of. In time she came back to the family and today is living a victorious Christian life. Prayer is our power and the key to total victory!

🖎 Take on the whole armor of God! Read aloud those verses from Ephesians 6, then take authority over your crisis. We must become aggressive and persistent in prayer, not giving up until the answer comes.

🖎 Give up in yourself! The first step from the "twelve step" programs for addictions and dysfunctional relationships is to admit your powerlessness (apart from prayer).

SAY IT IN SONG:

"I surrender all.
I surrender all.
All to thee, my Blessed Savior,
I surrender all."

Judson W. Van De Venter[6]

SOMETHING TO THINK ABOUT:

"In a time lacking in truth and certainty and filled with anguish and despair, no woman should be shamefaced in attempting to give back to the world, through her work, a portion of its lost heart."

Louise Bogan
Poet

LET'S PRAY:

Father, how could I have been so arrogant, so presumptuous, so filled with pride, that I thought I could chart my own course, live my own life and follow my own footsteps without asking for Your guidance, direction and most importantly, Your will? Forgive me, Lord, and put me on the right pathway again, following Your footsteps and doing Your work, which is the only way I want to live. In Jesus' precious name I pray. Amen.

Unraveled

Pictures

FOUR

New Beginnings:

Betsy looked into her mirror and examined the new wrinkles which seemingly spread in all directions before her eyes. She stood back and attempted to sing a high-C note, but her professional vibrato broke and echoed the imperfections through the empty halls of her home.

Long ago Betsy had determined to fill her life with people and win to Christ those she befriended. But that morning she realized that most of her friends, whether they walked with the Lord or not, were ignorant of Scripture and of the Christian life. As she stood feeling old and alone, she made a new decision. A friend had urged her to start a ladies' Bible study, and by coincidence a well-respected Bible teacher had offered to teach. She decided she'd do it.

A month later Betsy's house was spotless, her clothing and hair perfect, as she sat in her living room waiting for the doorbell to chime—with no premonition of what she was starting. As women streamed through the door that night, she rejoiced like a new bride and smiled nonstop for three hours. Her joy was even greater when a young career woman surrendered her life to Jesus Christ. Immediately fifteen of the women made the Bible study a priority on their calendars.

Every week Betsy invites new women to the Bible study. Daily she counsels them, helping with careers, love-lives, makeup—the works. Seasonally she opens the group to men for "parties," at which soul-winning is the goal.

One recent Wednesday night when her house was silent, she climbed into bed with the memory of the laughter of guests ringing in her ears and expectantly prayed over the next week. Then she thanked God that on this special day, her birthday, she felt she was living an abundant life for the first time ever—a fitting accomplishment at age seventy.

MEDITATION:

"And we all, with unveiled face, beholding the glory of the Lord, are being changed into his likeness from one degree of glory to another." 2 Corinthians 3:18 RSV

ACTION STEPS:

❧ If you are breathing while you read this page, God is not finished with you! Age and circumstance have nothing to do with God's plan for your life. He called Moses at eighty, Betsy at seventy—who knows how He will use you?

❧ You can be assured God is going to use you if you have a surrendered heart and mind. What He didn't ask you to do some time ago He may ask of you now. Whatever you believe He wants you to do, share it with two or three respected friends who will tell you if they think it is right, and keep praying. Once you have the "green light," go after it with all your might!

❧ You already know you know more than most other people, whether it's the announcer on the nightly news, the talk show host or the people you read about in books and newspapers. Don't let that wisdom go to waste! Be creative in ways of helping others with what you have to offer.

M Y   H U S B A N D   S A Y S :

"You're never too old, never too young, for God to use you."

"God never quits on you; don't quit on God."

T H E Y   S A Y :

"I keep the telephone of my mind open to peace, harmony, health, love and abundance. Then whenever doubt, anxiety, or fear try to call me, they keep getting a busy signal and soon they'll forget my number."

Edith Armstrong

"God does not ask your ability or your inability. He asks only your availability."

Mary Kay Ash
Businesswoman

Empty Nest:

A New Routine

"**D**on't forget to call, Sissy."

Karen walked slowly to the window as Sissy dashed onto the plane destined for college. *My last one gone*, Karen thought as she watched the plane taxi to the runway.

She returned home to find the house strange, where an eerie quiet reigned. Through the silence she could hear ghostly sounds of children's shouts, doors slamming, ringing laughter and stereos turned up too loud.

Her throat constricted and her eyes filled with tears. She swallowed. *Mustn't dwell on it.*

She had errands to run, so out she ran. Returning, she put away groceries bought carefully to feed only one. She was unable to cook. She turned on the television and ate a TV dinner. Preparing for bed that night, self-pity thumped so loudly in her chest she could hear it. *How many days 'til they come home for Christmas?*

Weeks passed. Routine things didn't make sense. The house didn't need as much cleaning—floors, laundry, kitchen. She talked to people more—clerks, cashiers, neighbors.

Sissy called for the third time, still vibrant, excited. Karen found it would have been easier to hear her depressed, needing her mother. She didn't.

Karen went into the kitchen, prepared a small casserole and popped it in the oven. *I gave my children life. They will not live it better than me!*

She pulled a tablet of paper out of the drawer and sat at the breakfast bar to make a list. "To do" on Mondays, Tuesdays.... Goals for this month. Goals by Christmas. Goals for one year from now. Rummaging around, she found the community recreation directory. Beginners' Oil Painting classes on Tuesday nights. *That's what I've always wanted to learn!* Excitement grew along with the list. Conversational French—that sounds interesting. And I have more time now to help at church.

Excitement bubbled up within her. Self-pity dissolved as a brand new routine took shape. Outlets opened. Latent talents arose. By the time the oven buzzer heralded the finished casserole, one season of life had passed into another.

MEDITATION:

"Be sure of this—that I am with you always, even to the end of the world." Matthew 28:20 TLB

ACTION STEPS:

❧ You only have twenty-four precious hours in each day, and not one is intended for self-pity. When you are lonely, you need intimate companionship—that's what friends are for. Call one. If you don't have one, make one! Thousands of lonely people live within miles of you, just waiting to meet you.

❧ When your routine is upset, you need new goals—that's what lists are for. Make one with God's help. Goals are just dreams with a date on them. Pray and ask God for a goal for today. For this week. For this month. For this year. Post it on a bathroom mirror, bedroom door, coffee pot or any place where you'll see it every day. As you work toward those goals, God will give you other projects and desires will spring from them, branching in new directions for you to explore. Without forcing it, your life will become full again in ways you never dreamed, and you will be continuing to fulfill God's plan for your life.

THINK IT OVER:

"Don't shut yourself up in a bandbox because you are a woman, but understand what is going on, and educate yourself to take part in the world's work for it all affects you and yours."

Louisa May Alcott
Writer

LET'S PRAY:

Father, what do You have for me now? I'm listening. Help me step into this new time with eagerness and boldness. In Jesus' name. Amen.

Loneliness:

What do you say to a woman after her young husband suddenly dies of a brain tumor and leaves her almost penniless with three small children?

When loved ones leave for the evening, a weekend or a month, we long to be joyously reunited. But when we are separated through death, disappearance or abandonment, loneliness can attach itself to us like an unwanted limb.

Such painful loneliness is part of the period of grief, which often includes feeling rejected and angry at the person who is gone, and sometimes at God. But beyond the grief, there is life and hope in Jesus, who draws us to our heavenly Father.

Life on earth is imperfect—a shadow of the joys of eternity to come. Each person shares a measure of loneliness even in the happiest circumstances, because God has placed eternity in our hearts. We long for timelessness and total loving intimacy with God, which will be ours in heaven.

Not every widow has a story like this young woman's. After her husband's death, she prayerfully pushed up her sleeves and went to work to provide for her children. Time passed and one evening she had a strong impression to go to a specific restaurant for dinner. There she met the man she later married. A seemingly ordinary coincidence, and yet extraordinary because God orchestrated it.

When you worship God, He draws you to Himself in intimate relationship, which eases loneliness. It foreshadows what we were created for—to spend eternity with Him. Then He'll give you something to do. And through it all, God is faithful. Not all widows remarry, nor do they all want to. But whatever is best for your life, you can be sure God will provide it when you trust Him.

MEDITATION:

"For salvation comes from God. What joys he gives to all his people." Psalm 3:8 TLB

ACTION STEPS:

❧ If you know someone who has recently lost an important person, or is given to episodes of deep loneliness or depression, consider making a "Blessing Book" for them. Get a scrapbook or photo album and gather remembrances of blessings from their life—a child's school picture, a picture or advertisement for something they owned together, a photo of the flowers they once gave you, a bulletin or program from a service or special event you attended together, and vacation momentos. It will mean the world to them.

❧ Do something wonderful for another person. Get your mind off your loneliness by considering others. Think of those closest to you first, then move into the community—the senior center, rest home, homeless shelter, home for unwed mothers or suicide prevention center. Why not? You are very much alive and God has not finished with you yet!

❧ Prayer, the kind where we allow God to envelope us with His love and acceptance, is the greatest antidote to loneliness.

Once you feel His closeness in the Spirit, ask Him for a friend with whom you can share life in the physical.

A WOMAN'S WISDOM:

"Those who do not know how to weep with their whole heart don't know how to laugh either."

Golda Meir
Prime Minister,
Israel

LET'S PRAY:

Oh Father, I remember You promised You would never leave me and Your faithfulness gives me courage for this time. Show me Your plan and lead me in Your path. I ask this in Jesus' name. Amen.

Solo Meals:

My morning coffee and toast were warm and pleasant when a "squawk!" outside the kitchen window drew my attention to a small flock of yellow-breasted birds, which had suddenly descended on my back yard. They hopped about the grass, pecked at apparently delicious morsels and talked to each other. "What a sweet family," I thought, as I returned to my lone placemat and dish. Their company cheered me as I continued my least favorite activity—eating alone.

Solo dining has become a fact of life in our society. In many busy families, Dad may eat late, children early, and Mom eats after everyone else is finished. Children then move away, leaving parents to break bread in solitude.

Many things separate us, but we would do well to follow the birds' example and bring our family together to share a meal. Gathering loved ones around the dining table (with the television OFF!) and engaging in conversation gives parents the ability to influence their children and grandchildren. Most of the world's great leaders recall family mealtime as a highlight of their formative years. One of the side benefits is that when we eat with others, we are more apt to eat a nutritious meal.

Some people, on the other hand, do well with solo dining. My daughter, for one, lived alone in Japan for more than a year, where her only English-speaking companions were books. She liked to prepare a nice meal for herself, turn on some soothing music, and dive into a classic book. She turned such occasions for loneliness into celebrations of fine food and literature.

As I ate in solitude that morning, I was thankful for my food, for the birds that warmed me and for the sweet memories I had of lovely family mealtimes. I longed to show someone those little birds, yet I was grateful I was able to see and appreciate them myself. I pulled a book toward me, left open from the night before, and when I next looked up my little friends had taken wing and only crumbs remained of my breakfast.

MEDITATION:

"Therefore I say unto you, Take no thought for your life, what ye shall eat, or what ye shall drink; nor yet for your body, what ye shall put on. Is not the life more than meat, and the body than raiment? Behold the fowls of the air: for they sow not, neither do they reap, nor gather into barns; yet your heavenly Father feedeth them. Are ye not much better than they?" Matthew 6:25,26

ACTION STEPS:

❧ Books make good companions, provided you cultivate living friendships as well. Once I was invited into the old family house of an aristocratic British couple. I was surprised to see that running down each wall of their formal dining room were two shelves stocked with books. Keeping a library of books on a shelf next to your table sounds reasonable if you want to keep your mind active when you find yourself without a companion.

❧ When alone, a good sacred music tape or the Bible on tape makes great company. Keep a tape player on your table and turn it on so you can literally chew on every word!

🐦 A well-known traveling minister once told me that eating alone was the one thing he didn't like about traveling. In hotel restaurants, before he sat down he would see if any other men were alone, then ask to sit with them. This almost always resulted in a lively conversation which did wonders to assuage his lonely feelings.

🐦 Children develop their food choices by what parents serve them, so balancing our diets is vital for more than just ourselves. Failure to eat properly hurts our bodies and minds, and ultimately can hinder our spirits. Watch what fuel you give your body. When we eat alone, it is easy to eat poorly. Eat as often as possible with friends who will hold you accountable to good stewardship of your health.

FOOD FOR THOUGHT:

"He ate and drank the precious words,
His spirit grew robust;
He knew no more that he was poor,
Nor that his frame was dust.
He danced along the dingy days,
And this bequest of wings
Was but a book. What liberty
A loosened spirit brings!"

Emily Dickinson[7]
Poet

"What a commentary on civilization, when being alone is considered suspect; when one has to apologize for it, make excuses, hide the fact that one practices it—like a secret vice."

Anne Morrow Lindbergh
Writer

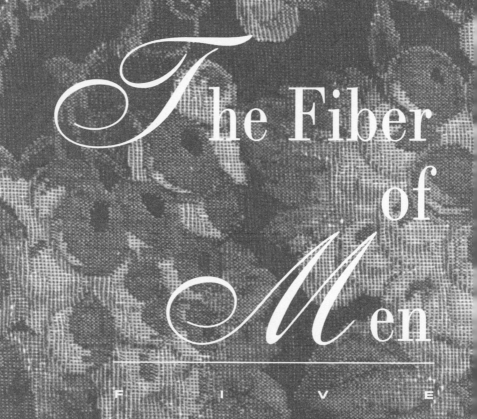

The Fiber of Men

FIVE

Differences:

Isn't it a bother to marry someone unlike yourself? Yet differences are part of God's plan for His universe. It takes varying notes to create beautiful harmonies and many colors to make a rainbow. Still, we often have a negative response to dissimilarities, especially in marriage.

Take morning people and night people, for example. Morning people seem to take literally Proverbs 20:13 that says, "Love not sleep, lest thou come to poverty." Bible stories back up their claim to the superiority of getting up in the wee hours. David rose early to pray. Samuel's parents rose early to worship. Job was up early to offer sacrifices to the Lord.

I admit morning people have a good argument. It's just that my idea of early is 7:30 a.m., not 5:00 a.m. If I have to, I can beat the sun out of bed, but I'd rather let the sun get a good hold on the day before I start mine.

To my husband, however, nothing is more glorious than the sunrise. He starts every day at dawn with a positively chipper attitude. Sometimes I quote Proverbs 27:14 to him in jest, "He that blesseth his friend with a loud voice, rising early in the morning, it shall be counted a curse to him." To make it worse, he also likes to go to sleep early. Last night he was in bed before dark.

Years have passed and by God's grace we've learned to coordinate. I plan the evening get-togethers with friends. He plans the early meetings and flights. So I keep us socializing in the evenings and he keeps us working in the mornings. In spite of ourselves, we're a team!

There is a true saying, "God makes you different to make you one." When we recognize, accept and learn to appreciate the differences, we can create beautiful harmony in our homes.

MEDITATIONS:

"As iron sharpens iron, so a man sharpens the countenance of his friend." Proverbs 27:17 NKJV

"For as in one body we have many members, and all the members do not have the same function...Having gifts that differ according to the grace given to us, let us use them." Romans 12:4,6 RSV

"If you shout a pleasant greeting to a friend too early in the morning, he will count it as a curse." Proverbs 27:14 TLB

"If you love sleep, you will end in poverty. Stay awake, work hard, and there will be plenty to eat!" Proverbs 20:13 TLB

ACTION STEPS:

❧ Are you and your husband opposites? A bit of giving on both sides, plus a good dose of humor, helps. It's good to see how the differences complement each other. Concentrate today on how you enhance each other's lives. Does one of you conserve money to prepare for the future, while the other spends it easily to enjoy today? Does one enjoy music and constant noise while the other appreciates quiet? Do you experience things together, yet see them through completely different eyes? As you look at how the other enhances or balances your life, write down your findings. Then do the same tomorrow, and the next day. By the end of the month, you'll have a journal of how your lives enrich each other's, which you can meditate on instead of thinking constantly about how aggravating the differences are.

❧ Differences often grate on us, causing us to insist on having our own way, blinding us to others' perceptions. One way is not necessarily right or better than another, or else God would have created only one personality. Become grateful for differences that keep variety in life. Spend a morning in prayer, telling God you forgive your spouse or other family members for everything they have done that annoyed you. Thank God for every difference, large or small. Develop an appreciation for differences and an attitude of thankfulness for the variety your family provides.

WISELY PUT:

"We all live with the objective of being happy; our lives are all different and yet the same."

Anne Frank,
Diarist

"It would be a thousand pities if women wrote like men, or lived like men, or looked like men, for if two sexes are quite inadequate, considering the vastness and variety of the world, how should we manage with one only?"

Virginia Woolf
Writer

JUST FOR FUN:

"In society it is etiquette for ladies to have the best chairs and get handed things. In the home the reverse is the case. That is why ladies are more sociable than gentlemen."

Virginia Graham
Author

Careers:

In today's economy a historical shift has caused many women to capture high-paying jobs while some men in middle management can barely feed a family. As a result, most women work and many earn more than their husbands. Likewise, many single women earn more than their potential suitors.

A woman named Debbie wrote me a letter describing her resentment about her husband's failure in business. She had become their family's main provider. Yet her husband prayed with his family, attended church regularly and was in all other respects a good husband and father.

Debbie's complaint brought to mind at least a half dozen of my female friends who were the main providers for their families. I immediately called one, Judi, and explained Debbie's situation. Judi said she would give anything if her husband would pray with her family as Debbie's did. She said her husband did not have a career, nor a grasp on his role in the family. Judi was grateful that at least she had earning power during this bleak period of their lives.

Then I heard Dr. Ernestine Reems at a women's seminar. She said she had counseled successful women who were unwilling to marry a good man because he was "only" a janitor or clerk. She reasoned with them that even if he hadn't graduated from college or didn't make as much money, he was still a good man. After all, no one wants to earn money only to spend it all alone. We'd all rather spend our time and money with someone we love. Her advice, given in dynamic fashion:

"Take the money *and* the honey!"

Priorities are first spiritual, then love of others, then practical, although the practical issues are often what plague us. Debbie's Christian husband wasn't a perfect one, yet he had taken care of the first priority. Judi's husband had done none of them, but her grateful attitude made her situation tolerable.

While we strive for the ideal, we live the real. If we are resentful when we don't reach the ideal, we'll miss the joys of the real.

MEDITATION:

"The man who finds a wife finds a good thing; she is a blessing to him from the Lord." Proverbs 18:22 TLB

ACTION STEPS:

❧ List your husband's positive attributes in your journal or on a piece of paper. Remember, whatever attracted you to him in the first place is still there. Draw out those qualities spiritually by praying for him, then speak about them to him in conversation. Every time you want to point out his failures, look instead for a success and compliment him.

❧ You cannot catch flies with vinegar. You cannot have a happy marriage nor build up your husband with criticism. If you are critical, make a point to stop criticizing for one day. Then try again tomorrow. Soon you'll have broken a bad habit.

❧ Thank God for your husband and tell him you love him at least once a day.

❧ When your husband accomplishes something in the work force, perhaps just applying for a new job, let him know how proud you are of him. Speak words of discouragement to God privately; speak words of encouragement to your husband openly.

GOOD POINT:

"Success is important only to the extent that it puts one in a position to do more things one likes to do."

Sarah Caldwell
Conductor

"Some people are more turned on by money than they are by love…In one respect, they're alike. They're both wonderful as long as they last."

Abigail Van Buren
Advice Columnist

"It's easy to be independent when you've got money. But to be independent when you haven't got a thing—that's the Lord's test."

Mahalia Jackson
Singer

upport:

My husband received an anonymous letter that I would have loved to have answered. The writer could have been the wife of any strong man or leader. Her complaint was a desperate concern to find her way in life while feeling inadequate next to her husband.

Being a leader's wife, I admit I have felt the same, particularly when other wives I've known appear to be towering talents. When Edwin was pastoring, we once lived in an area where the pastors' wives around me excelled in music, teaching and ministry. My abilities seemed dwarfed next to theirs.

In this woman's letter I could feel her insecurity. She believed everyone was more accomplished and she allowed that thought to breed resentment, which created jealousy—of others and of her husband. She felt hurt when people were drawn to her husband and not to her. She didn't understand that everyone—male or female—does their best for someone they admire, and that men and women alike gravitate toward strong men.

The wife of a leader must cast off these feelings and create openness and affection between her and her mate by giving of herself to meet his needs spiritually, mentally and physically. The only alternatives are to ask him to stop whatever he does or to leave him—not good options! Short of abuse or misuse, "'Til death do us part!" is every spouse's anthem.

I give any wife these five tips:

1. Let your husband's competition arise from others, not you. Don't try to squeeze into his position.

2. Keep focused on who God made you to be. Don't emulate others.

3. Develop your skills—which your worries may blind you to right now.

4. Hold tightly to your commitment. Don't make a mockery of your marriage by divorcing.

5. Keep a strong prayer and Bible life. Unlike anything else, prayer and meditation on the Word will renew perspective and rejuvenate you.

It would be wonderful if the writer of that letter would read this! Someone said, "You read to know you are not alone." Surely she is not alone, and neither are you. Others have blazed the trail, so just follow the steps and find your way.

M E D I T A T I O N :

"A wise woman *builds* her house." Proverbs 14:1 TLB (emphasis mine)

A C T I O N   S T E P S :

❧ Opening yourself with a generous and loving heart to soothe the pains of other women may help conquer the pains of jealousy and feelings of inadequacy. People are far more alike than we think. Such feelings are felt by everyone at one time or another. We live in a needy world. When you can help some-one have one less need, that's a success. Solve another's need and you're as successful as anyone.

☙ Give yourself a good self-examination:

How is your side of the relationship with your husband?

Is he first (except for the Lord) in your life, or is self-pity number one?

Do you help him feel like a whole person?

Is your home a heaven or a hell for him?

Does he have to fight off your hostility and condemnation?

Take these to the Lord in prayer. Have enough courage to look at yourself with His help. When you honestly bare your heart before God, He will show you what to work on. If you lack anything, it will be given to you by your loving Father. Be sure to make insecurity a specific matter of prayer too.

☙ If possible, take a vacation together—just the two of you—and get to know each other all over again.

T R U T H :

"Getting along with men isn't what's truly important. The vital knowledge is how to get along with a man, one man."
Phyllis McGinley
Writer, Poet

"Remember, no one can make you feel inferior without your consent."

Eleanor Roosevelt
Writer,
Humanitarian,
U. N. Delegate,
First Lady

Separation:

"**G**ood-by, Dear. I love you. I'll be praying for you."

I shut the front door as my husband got in the car to drive to the airport. This trip would be three whole weeks.

The car sped away.

Alone.

Sensing the long void ahead is disconcerting. A thick silence falls on the house and I know I must break it before it consumes me. I sing a worshipful chorus. I settle into my chair and celebrate the solitude with prayer and my Bible.

Despondency nips at my heels, aiming to rob me of the joy God provides. I resist. Without the Lord's joy how can I accomplish what He has for me today? What does He have for me? Laziness knocks. Drowsiness threatens.

I rouse myself and begin the most obvious tasks. Being alone only magnifies things left undone. I plunge into projects I've avoided. Once I am working I feel better. A friend calls on the telephone. Before I realize what has happened I have been able, with God's help, of course, to show her a way out of a problematic situation that she is in. My heart is lifted up.

The joys of small accomplishments replace the pangs of loneliness.

The day closes, but my mind is too active to sleep. After I complete some letters I rest my head and am reminded of God's words, "I will never leave you nor forsake you" (See Hebrews 13:5).

The new day dawns and my list grows instead of shortens. I find a few minutes to call a friend. We talk and laugh and suddenly I have a lunch date. My daughter-in-law calls and now I have a dinner date too. Church is tomorrow. Anticipating precious camaraderie erases the last bit of self-pity.

Monday I make dreaded appointments—dentist, ophthalmologist. I return the warranty item that broke three months ago. I read my homeowner's insurance policy. I call the agent. Another appointment. Every day fills up.

My husband returns, happy to see that I am relaxed, not anxious. We go out for dinner and I tell him my achievements. He gives me highlights. A dozen projects are put off for another time.

MEDITATION:

"I will never leave thee, nor forsake thee." Hebrews 13:5

ACTION STEPS FOR WORK AND SPORTS "WIDOWS":

❧ Who would appreciate your company or need your help most? Does the church secretary need a hand? No one wants a busybody, but everyone wants a blessing. Perhaps someone needs you to run errands, or an elderly person would love a trip to the local cafeteria. Better yet, your teenage child or grandchild could benefit from having your attention solely on him or her.

❧ If you find yourself alone, turn off the television and get busy! Once you begin to be productive, endless possibilities present themselves. When was the last time you—

walked the neighborhood

painted your bedroom

visited your aunt

cleaned the baseboards

had a good workout

reviewed your gifts and offerings

hosed off the front porch

trimmed the rose bushes

balanced your checkbook

shopped for a better bank

wrote to your best friends

called your sister

wrote a poem

sat on your back porch drinking tea with a good book

ordered Christmas cards

prayed out loud all of the 150 psalms (whew!)

contacted social security to check your contributions

adjusted your household budget

browsed in a good bookstore

tried a new recipe

walked the mall

investigated a computer store

took a community class

went to the dentist

attended a weekend seminar

played at a pet shop

serviced your car

bought an interesting tape series

celebrated a friend's birthday

got your cat a check-up

tried a new restaurant

planned a special dinner

wrote your husband a love letter?

THOUGHTFULLY PUT:

"I never notice what has been done. I only see what remains to be done."

Marie Curie
Physician, Scientist

"If I can stop one heart from breaking,
I shall not live in vain:
If I can ease one life the aching,
Or cool one pain,
Or help one fainting robin
Unto his nest again,
I shall not live in vain."

Emily Dickinson[8]
Poet

LET'S PRAY:

Father, help me sense Your presence today and order my path. I'm looking for Your possibilities and trusting Your promises. In Jesus' name. Amen.

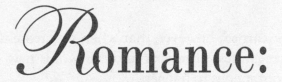

Romance:

Edwin and I looked at each other and smiled with appreciation and enjoyment. The crowd around us was cheering the team, carrying us back in memory to our first date when he took me to a UCLA football game. As we left the stadium hand in hand, I don't know what people thought—after all, we've now been married forty-some years.

My grandchildren squeal and my children laugh when Edwin and I spontaneously break into a little dance in the kitchen, peck each other's cheek, hold hands as we walk or harmonize on some old tune from years gone by. These are silly things, yet they are important reminders of our love for each other. Edwin tells men to say to their wives every day, "You are God's gift to me. I love you." We wives need to say something similar to our husbands or better yet, show them.

Edwin and I have learned that romance is not something you "fall" into, nor is it necessarily planned, nor is it the result of wild emotional passion. Instead, romance is an expression of love, whether spontaneous or planned, emotional or practical. Romance is something Edwin and I build daily by appreciating each other and letting each other know it.

I was a little embarrassed the first time Edwin told a flight attendant, "We're on our honeymoon." It's a little crazy because he says it regardless of where we're going, on business or for pleasure. I've learned, however, that when we create that loving atmosphere, regardless of how absurd our words may sound, we invite the spontaneous to happen.

Since we often travel, which could become grueling drudgery, sometimes we find an hour or two when we scan the shops or try new foods—anything we don't usually do at home. We've also checked the newspaper and ended up at concerts and sporting events. Without a bit of advance planning, we've gone everywhere from Wimbledon to the Watergate hearings. It's fun! And sharing experiences makes our love feel fresh again.

On this evening we found ourselves at a football game, where the crowd seemed to warm our own feelings for one another. When you practice romance every day, each new spontaneous expression makes it "grand."

MEDITATIONS:

"Anxiety in a man's heart weighs it down, but a kind word makes it glad." Proverbs 12:25 MLB

"Above all else, guard your affections. For they influence everything else in your life." Proverbs 4:23 TLB

"Honor goes to kind and gracious women...." Proverbs 11:16 TLB

ACTION STEPS:

❧ Get some greeting cards or make some "love notes" for your husband today. Put a "sticky" in his newspaper that says you love him, or a note on his mirror that says you're going to stick closer to him than aftershave. Edwin sometimes leaves me greeting cards around the house—under my pillow, in the fridge. Before he goes away, I've hidden cards in his luggage, one in the suit I know he will wear, another in the folds of clothes or in his shoes.

  Do something romantic today. Plan something for tomorrow. Then for the next day. Even stagnant love cannot resist such nurturing. Anyone can settle into a routine that becomes dull. Break the routine! Pack up a picnic dinner and take it to a park, or go for a ride in the country. Wear his favorite perfume, cook his favorite food even when it's not his birthday.

  Sometimes romance is hindered by a lack of common courtesy. Work toward unity by listening to him respectfully when he speaks, not criticizing him in front of others, and keeping communication lines open.

  Touching doesn't need to be limited to the bedroom. We don't need long, passionate kisses to show warmth and express love. The daily little hugs and kisses are warm renewals of our love and commitment to each other. The intimate feeling of holding hands never grows wearisome. Every expression of love builds into grand romance.

  Have trouble getting him warmed up to romance? Try meeting his needs first. A friend of my daughter's wrote out "Weekly Accountabilities" for their accountability group partners to tape to their bathroom mirrors—and follow! You could type this out and do the same:

Did you *encourage* your husband this week?

Did you *support* your husband this week?

Did you *submit* to your husband this week?

Did you *respect* your husband this week?

Did you *love* your husband this week?

You may not always *feel* like doing or being these things for your husband each day. Regardless of whether *he* is doing *his* part, *you* are still responsible to do *yours*. God holds us accountable and *expects* us to be the wives He created us to be, *in spite* of each day's circumstances.

NUGGETS:

"A woman should, I think, love her husband better than anything on earth except her own soul, which I think a man should respect above everything on earth but his own soul; and there my dear is a very pretty puzzle for you, which a good many people have failed to resolve."

> Fanny Kemble
> Actress

JUST FOR FUN:

"An archaeologist is the best husband a woman can have; the older she gets, the more interested he is in her."

> Agatha Christie
> Writer

Late Life Love:

"I've had it!" were the last words Dorothy heard her husband say. Left with three small children, she felt lost and humiliated. The divorce proceedings were so painful that she inwardly vowed never to date or look at another man.

She took up secretarial work to provide for her family. In time, she was able to buy a house in a small community and soon made many friends. As the children grew, she found time to take up pottery, painting and start a small business on the side.

At work, each of Dorothy's bosses found her indispensable. Her attitude was positive, her work precise to the smallest detail. With promotions and raises, Dorothy's quality of life continued to rise along with her self-esteem. Her life was full and satisfying.

Years passed, the children had their own families, and Dorothy decided to retire. She figured out how to sell her house, move closer to her brothers and sisters, and still live comfortably. Once accomplished, she started again to find ways to become valuable to her new community, as she had been back home.

Tennis always interested her, although she was not very athletic, so the newspaper advertisement for beginner adult classes intrigued her enough to attend on the first day. She tried to look her youngest, showing up in white shorts, but she was carrying what she found out later was a ridiculously outdated racquet.

"I remember those!" an older man said and laughed with her at the dead give-away of her age. Sure enough, they were the two oldest people in the class and instantly gravitated toward each other.

When she went home that night, she could not stop thinking about this man, her first new friend. As she lay in bed that night, suddenly she gasped. She realized she was interested in him. Quickly throwing the covers back and kneeling beside her bed, she tried to repent, but could not find the words. *What did I do wrong to repent of*, she wondered.

Then it hit her. She had long since forgotten the vow she made to herself, and without realizing it, over the years God had healed her of the bitterness and emotion which were behind that vow. Now she repented for ever making such a rash vow.

Within weeks, life surprised her and she walked down an aisle in a little chapel to make a brand new vow of marriage.

MEDITATIONS:

"God setteth the solitary in families." Psalm 68:6

"The Lord tears down the house of the proud, but He protects the boundries of the widow." Proverbs 15:25 MLB

ACTION STEPS:

❧ Do you think your life is over? Become active! Do you think you could never attract a man? Quit thinking about it, be the very best you can be, and you'll be shocked at how many people are attracted to you! Do you regret the past? Cut off those negative thoughts and live today for all it's worth right where you are!

❧ Unlike Dorothy, some women never stop trying to make a play for men. Usually this starts early in life with some sense of rejection from a father figure or boyfriend. Then we spend a lifetime trying to make up for it. Forget about it! If you constantly think about men, take those thoughts captive, as the Bible says, to the knowledge of Jesus Christ. Worrying about how men perceive you and striving to be attractive to them is a substitute for a living, vital relationship with our Heavenly Father, our man of all men. He said He will be the "husband" to the woman without one. Let Him be your husband and best friend today!

❧ You can become a "clique" of just one person when you refuse to go out with others and socialize. It is self-centered not to share all you have and know with people placed in your path. Get out today and greet at least one person with warm enthusiasm. Then find one tomorrow, and after you've made that a habit, step it up to two or three.

LOVE NOTES:

> *"Life is a stream*
> *On which we strew*
> *Petal by petal the flower of our heart...."*
>
> Amy Lowell[9]
Poet and Writer

"He simply said my name."

Edna O'Brien
Writer

"I will always be grateful for my public-park beginning in tennis. One learned many bad habits in tennis, but one learned to play against all kinds of players and against all odds."

Alice Marble
Tennis Player

LET'S PRAY:

Father, I know Your plans for me are only for good. I'm committing my heart to You for healing and restoration. I release the future into Your care. In Jesus' name I pray. Amen.

Ties That Bind

SIX

Children:

GROWING A FAMILY

Like growing a garden, raising children is a difficult kind of joy. Mothers generally come to the task without prior training or household help. Maybe we rocked our baby brother or babysat, but Mom did the rest. For most of us, launching into twenty-four-hour-a-day care is a consuming task.

Once we adjust to tilling the soil of our young child's life, we can become so focused on the work that we don't see the child's character taking root. Suddenly seeing him or her grow in ways beyond our control can be worrisome. Like after trimming the roses to perfection, we find that weeds sprang up in the morning glories.

Most mothers want their children to develop godly virtues. Perhaps we dream of our son as the next Billy Graham or our daughter as another Madam Curie. Then we find them disobeying or lying and our world caves in. That's where we need perspective and faith in God.

Young Janet came to me because her son's report card grades were lowered for an "unsatisfactory" attitude. "I guess I'll just have to face it," Janet sobbed, "I have a problem child."

While her concern was justified, I knew her son was not a problem child. I encouraged her to meet the boy's teacher. During the meeting the teacher assured Janet the problem with her son's grades was due to forgetting to do assignments and not studying—more an organizational problem than a character flaw.

We can easily lose sight of the good growth taking hold in our children by focusing on the negatives, much like struggling over one little weed in our garden and failing to see the rows of gorgeous flowers. If you are doing your best, you may need to lay down your tools, sit back and look down that row. We only work the field. God grows the plants.

MEDITATION:

"Then our sons in their youth will be like well-nurtured plants, and our daughters will be like pillars carved to adorn a palace." Psalm 144:12 NIV

ACTION STEPS:

❧ List your children's strengths. Then prayerfully write down ways you can help them change any weaknesses into strengths. Allow God to do the work as you pray over these. If bringing up their weaknesses could be disheartening, make them only a matter of prayer, not discussion.

❧ If you still have small children, or are raising or helping to raise grandchildren, try sitting down with them and going over recent events. Discuss what they can change and what they are doing right. Accent the positive. Let them know that whatever they do, you love them and are concerned for their welfare. Make appointments with them often so your job doesn't become one of constant correction. Get the jump on difficulties by giving them the opportunity to "fess up" before they're "found out."

❧ Children are not raised just to become independent adults. Adult children need nurturing and encouragement throughout their lives. Choose your words carefully so you're not meddling, and apologize often if anything you say could be construed as such. When you have teenagers, the more you bite your tongue on all that you *could* say, the more impact you will have with what you *do* say.

THEY KNOW:

"The business of the husbandman is not to waste his endeavors in seeking to make his orchard attain the strength and majesty of his forest, but to rear each to the perfection of its nature."

Emma Hart Willard
Educator

"The giving of love is an education in itself."

Eleanor Roosevelt
Writer,
Humanitarian,
U. N. Delegate,
First Lady

In-Laws:

A s a single girl, I didn't spend much time thinking about marriage. But I knew I would have to be comfortable with whomever I married, and he would have to share the same values my parents taught me.

Once I married and had my own children, I saw them take the characteristics of mine and Edwin's home, and look for someone who would share similar values. The result is that my children's spouses now express as much about Edwin, me, and our parents, as our children do.

Seeing the reflection of the generations in my children's families gives me great satisfaction. I must admit, however, that I want to believe some of the characteristics of my children's partners are NOT the expression of the generations! Yet if my children love these people enough to marry them, who am I to pass judgment?

Although I did not always see eye-to-eye with my own mother-in-law, she did teach me how to be an in-law. When Edwin and I married, I didn't even know how to heat a can of soup. Mom painstakingly taught me to cook, wash clothes and iron a shirt. Then Edwin and I became Christians and launched into ministry. Mom had thirty years' experience on us there too. When she gave us "helpful" tips, I did not always take kindly to them.

Years have passed and I now see what Mom really did. She offered helpful advice, but there were many, many things we did wrong that she chose not to address at all. Instead she quietly prayed for us and never let us know she was aware of more flaws than those for which she gave counsel.

Part of creating a loving family is to overlook mistakes and take troublesome matters to God in prayer. Mom did not create unpleasant memories, but instead recognized words that were better left unspoken. Edwin and I have tried to do likewise.

In-laws are here to stay. Loving them is a way of loving our children and respecting the heritage of our grandchildren.

MEDITATION:

"Hatred stirs up strife, but love covers all sins." Proverbs 10:12 NKJV

ACTION STEPS:

❧ You may have an in-law "situation" that some loving care can cure. I encourage you not to let this day pass until you have prayed over the problem, then applied some love. For serious problems, you may need days of prayer before you are ready to talk to the person or write a letter. But you only live once, and family peace is worth the tiny sacrifice of time on our knees.

❧ In-laws are a special part of your family. After all, without them your family would never grow. And if something doesn't grow, it dies. Consider doing something special to appreciate your in-laws this year. Can you celebrate their birthdays in a new way? Or just send them each a card of appreciation.

❧ Sometimes besides regular Christmas gifts, Edwin buys all the guys the same electronic gadget or another "guy thing," and I buy all the girls something like gloves or perfume. When in-laws are treated equally, much goodwill is spread around.

WORDS OF WISDOM:

"No matter how many communes anybody invents, the family always creeps back."

Margaret Mead
Anthropologist

"Love is something like the clouds that were in the sky before the sun came out. You cannot touch the clouds, you know; but you feel the rain and know how glad the flowers and the thirsty earth are to have it after a hot day. You cannot touch love either; but you feel the sweetness that it pours into everything. Without love you would not be happy."

Annie Sullivan
Educator

Aging Parents:

I tiptoe into Mom's room. She is napping. When she is awake she constantly patrols the rest home—greeting people and asking nurses if they have work for her. She must be tired. She is ninety-one.

I look at her pictures on the wall, smiling, robust. For years she preached the gospel to down-and-outers in Los Angeles' skid row district. She also built churches, found pastors for them and preached or taught when needed. Twenty years ago she was still keeping up her land, one week trimming trees, another cementing the drainage ditch she dug. It never occurred to her that "Women don't do that." To her, nothing was impossible.

Two years ago she still lived alone. Today her body is in perfect health, but her energy is finally ebbing and her mind is confused. She became so confused we had to find this place for her, a safe home where she is well cared for.

Were she to awaken, she might not recognize me. She can't communicate much. Her conversation is made up of fragments of memories—some old, some new. When we sing, her mind won't allow her mouth to form the words, but her spirit soars. At times she claps her hands and moves to the rhythms. She moves her hands to lead the choir.

I watch her peaceful sleep. I am aware that she still possesses a healthy spirit. I lean over and lay my hand on her. Softly I pray. She stirs.

"Thank *You*, Jesus," she murmurs.

Regardless of the ravages of age, her spirit is still the strong, indomitable power that motivated a family for nine decades. Nothing can quench that spirit, not death nor devil nor disease. Mom is eternally bound to her Savior, intended to pass from this life to the next, but never to die.

MEDITATION:

"O God, You have taught me from my youth...I declared Your wondrous works. Yes, even when I am old and gray-headed, O God, forsake me not, *but* keep me alive until I have declared Your mighty strength to *this* generation." Psalm 71:17,18 AMP

ACTION STEPS:

&. Caring for parents when children still need care, watching a loved one fall prey to the ravages of disease, making decisions about another's life while keeping in mind what you and your family can tolerate—none of these are easy parts of life. Thank God He is with us through it all. Lift your eyes off your difficulties today and see the eternal Spirit realm unfold before you. God is God. Nothing will ever shake that. Faith in Him through His Son Christ Jesus will make and keep you strong.

&. God knows all and sees all. He knows what we are capable of, and when we need a break. When caring for others seems overwhelming, one of my favorite verses is, "You chart the path ahead of me, and tell me where to stop and rest" (Psalm 139:3 TLB). Did you miss one of His resting places? Take a load off your feet for fifteen minutes today, sit and do nothing or curl up with a book. God doesn't expect you to hold the universe! That's His job, and He will keep it going while you rest.

❧ Mom's rest home is the final harvest field. How I appreciate the churches and individuals who come to perform gospel services. The residents' faces glow as they sing the stirring hymns they grew up with. One more opportunity for those who have fallen away to know God. A wonderful place for families and groups of all ages to share God's love with those standing at the threshold of eternity.

GOOD POINT:

"It's better to light a candle than to curse the darkness."

Eleanor Roosevelt
Writer,
Humanitarian,
U. N. Delegate,
First Lady

JUST FOR FUN:

"Sure, I'm for helping the elderly. I'm going to be old myself someday."

Lillian Carter
President Carter's
Mother,
Nurse

Blended Families:

Stepparenting, or step-grandparenting, requires the patience of Sarah, the wisdom of Deborah, and the humor of Erma Bombeck. If parents go through "Parenting 101" with a new baby, people who become stepparents enter "Adventures in Parenting 2000"—a graduate course in persistence, love, determination, grace and forgiveness.

Worrisome situations begin almost from day one. A child moves into your home, or you into theirs, and they are suddenly thrust into the middle of your life. Yet they can become part of the warm family memories you'll retain for years if you can successfully merge your lives together.

Blending families from diverse educational and societal backgrounds is less a melting pot than a boiling caldron. To survive the heat, focus on the people themselves, not the circumstances. This is something we must do ourselves, not expect from others. Those of us with steprelatives must control ourselves to love unconditionally, give equally, root out resentment, forgive ex-spouses...and it is worth it!

My stepgrandsons have been alternately a trial and a blessing, but I would rather embrace them with their difficulties than lose them to someone or some place where we have no influence on them. We cannot allow disappointment, vengeance or anger to uproot our basic desire to see people—

especially family members—living in the Kingdom of God with all its benefits and eternal rewards.

Treat those stepchildren and stepgrandchildren as if they are your very own. Be concerned with their welfare, remember their birthdays, sympathize with their mistakes and give equally to relatives both natural born and acquired. Care enough to forgive and pray until all your family is headed for heaven. One day it will all come back to you—either as a worry and regret or a warm remembrance.

MEDITATION:

"Be strong and of good courage, do not fear or be in dread of them: for it is the Lord your God who goes with you: he will not fail you or forsake you." Deuteronomy 31:6 RSV

ACTION STEPS:

🕊 Using index cards, create one prayer card for each family member. Write their name on the top, then list their greatest needs, from your perspective as well as theirs. Each day pray over the person whose card is on top, then slip it to the back. This will continually bring to mind each person, as well as develop a good habit of prayer. When you cannot remember everyone each day, you'll rest assured knowing their card will come up soon.

🕊 Prayer produces intimacy. Praying for someone will iron out many, if not all, the wrinkles in the relationship, even if the other person doesn't participate.

🕊 Learn to love. Root out resentment daily in your prayer closet—not in an angry retort! Think of all the things that person is concerned about and pray for each. When we pray, we become genuinely interested in the answer to that prayer. Walking in another's shoes for awhile, even in prayer, will give you greater appreciation and patience, and eventually love.

❧ Lighten up and laugh! Program your mind to see errors as opportunities to laugh, not scold. If you do not naturally laugh easily, get some joke books or cassette tapes and set aside time each day to kick up your feet, throw back your head and just laugh.

SHE SAID IT:

"Having family responsibilities and concerns just has to make you a more understanding person."

Sandra Day O'Connor
U. S. Supreme
Court Justice

"Many people have said to me 'What a pity you had such a big family to raise. Think of the novels and the short stories and the poems you never had time to write because of that.' And I looked at my children and I said, 'These are my poems. These are my short stories.'"

Olga Masters
Writer

Stepmothers:

Today's abundance of broken homes glaringly illustrates how far we've moved from God's ideal for family relationships. Yet regardless of ideals, we must face circumstances realistically.

A close family friend will soon bring his bride, Brenda, into the home he shares with two teenaged daughters. He wisely sought counsel from mutual friends who gave Brenda a different picture of "family."

"They may not want you for their mother," our friend gently told Brenda. "Let the relationship develop naturally."

"Thank you for being honest," Brenda answered. "Everyone else said I needed to mother them."

Brenda's expectations could be mothering and family bliss, but her honeymoon could also be the shortest in history. Those daughters may be resentful, angry, or predisposed against her. Regardless of their outward smiles, inner urgings may be shouting:

"Why couldn't Dad stay with my real Mom?"

"I hate Mom for leaving and I'll hate my stepmom too."

"All my friends have problems with stepparents."

"Dad doesn't love me anymore."

Other issues arise. Mothers who raise children from birth know their likes and dislikes. A new stepchild may assume the new stepmom has the same knowledge, unwittingly creating certain failure for the stepmom. Or the child may feel shut out of the newlyweds' lives and use irksome antics to attract attention. The stepmother, on the other hand, may feel threatened by the child. With or without such undercurrents, it is unrealistic for complete strangers to treat one another immediately like family.

When troubles arise, we can depend on the Bible's basics to forgive, not return an angry comment, be patient and apply love liberally. How individuals express these may vary, but the elements are universal.

When we do our best, regardless of the outcome we live without regrets, which is an ideal all its own.

MEDITATIONS:

"But He said to me, My grace—My favor and loving-kindness and mercy—are enough for you, [that is, sufficient against any danger and to enable you to bear the trouble manfully]." 2 Corinthians 12:9 AMP

"Her children rise up and call her blessed." Proverbs 31:28 RSV

"If any of you lacks wisdom, let him ask of God...and it will be given to him." James 1:5 NKJV

ACTION STEPS:

❧ Through prayer, loving care, and frank talks with the children themselves, you may together be able to overcome most of the hurdles and settle into a peaceful routine of living. If you're the grandparent, do the same! The more family members work together, the smoother the blending will be.

❧ Work on your own expectations. Disappointment in life is not based on what we find, but on what we expect to find.

❧ Your relationship with your stepchildren, your new in-law or stepgrandchildren exists because of your relationship with a well-loved family member. Keep your primary relationship strong by sticking to biblical principles. For a husband, pray for him daily, forgive him, love and esteem him, prefer him to yourself, honor and respect him. Understand that the family member is in this as much as you are, with pressures and difficulties they may not yet have shared with you.

WORTH QUOTING:

"Some people are still unaware that reality contains unparalleled beauties. The fantastic and unexpected, the everchanging and renewing is nowhere so exemplified as in real life itself."

Berenice Abbott
Photographer

"You have to accept whatever comes and the only important thing is that you meet it with courage and with the best you have to give."

Eleanor Roosevelt
Writer,
Humanitarian,
U. N. Delegate,
First Lady

 Parenting:

A s Edwin dedicated the new church building for our home missions congregation, he tried to include everyone in the festivities. "Nancy and I are so happy you are here," he proudly announced. "We welcome you along with our children Paul, Lois, and—and— Nancy, what is our new baby's name?"

Retelling his faux pas has livened many a family dinner since then. With all our children, such parental mistakes were part and parcel of growing up.

We were new Christians when our first child was born and knew little about our new faith, but we knew we wanted our children to love God's Word and know Him in a personal way. While we made our share of mistakes, we also did some things right, and those are what have lasted.

In those early years we utilized church training and daily family prayer. We also tried to live our Christian faith in front of the children every day, to set an example of righteousness. We believed that we could do more by living out our Christianity than by thousands of spoken words. Regardless of how many mistakes we made, today all our children follow the Lord.

But what about the thousands of parents who become Christians later, or deepen their faith later, perhaps even after children grow to adulthood. What about the mistakes made? The opportunities lost? What about children whose hearts are hardened to the truth of the gospel?

The Bible has specific instructions:

1. Believe the promise of God that He will save your family. (Acts 16:31.)

2. Tell your children of your conversion. (Deuteronomy 6)

3. Ask them to forgive you for your shortcomings. (James 5:16; John 20:23)

4. Whenever you get a chance, don't preach, but share the love of God with them and show them His goodness to you. (1 John 4:7-11)

5. Be faithful in prayer. (Ephesians 6:18)

In many families, we may not see a mass conversion. But God is faithful, He is not willing that any, including your family, should perish (2 Peter 3:9). Stand on God's promises! Most importantly, accept Christ's provision to cover all your past mistakes. All parents make mistakes. That's one of the reasons we need Jesus!

MEDITATIONS:

"For all the promises of God in him are yea, and in him Amen, unto the glory of God by us." 2 Corinthians 1:20

"For as many as are the promises of God, they all find their Yes (answer) in Him (Christ). For this reason we also utter the Amen (so be it) to God through Him—that is, in His Person and by

His agency—to the glory of God." 2 Corinthians 1:20 AMP

"Believe on the Lord Jesus Christ, and thou shalt be saved, and thy house." Acts 16:31

ACTION STEPS:

❧ Be patient in the way God is patient with you. No one needs a Bible used like a club over their head. Use it like a loving message from a Father whose essence is love.

❧ In Matthew 15, we read the story about a woman pestering Jesus and His disciples. The disciples saw the situation from a human perspective. Their solution: Send her away. Often in our earthly thoughts we want bothersome people simply to go away—even our unsaved loved ones. Jesus could become impatient with us just like He could have with all of them. Instead, when the woman bothered Him again, He granted her request.

❧ Even the great man of God, Elijah, had to pray seven times to get an answer. There is something here for parents. *The Amplified Bible* says of the woman who pestered Jesus in Matthew 15:25 that she "kept praying." We can never let down. Never give up. Never back off. Not when we have children who don't yet know Jesus Christ or are backslid and running from God. Nothing is more worthy of our time and prayers than to see our own families won to Christ and serving Him.

ON GREAT MISTAKES:

"Every great mistake has a halfway moment, a split second when it can be recalled and perhaps remedied."

Pearl S. Buck
Author

"Be bold. If you're going to make an error, make a doozy, and don't be afraid to hit the ball."

Billy Jean King
Tennis Player

LET'S PRAY:

Father, I entrust my children to You. Thank You for keeping Your hand of protection over them. Your promise for salvation is for my entire household, so I rest in Your work. Send Your Spirit to draw them to You. In Jesus' name. Amen.

Responsibility:

I believe the most mature people I know are those who were given responsibility from the earliest of ages. Helping pick up toys at age two, cleaning their rooms, helping with the heavy housework as teenagers.

Some children are overburdened with ludicrous demands. One young friend of mine started keeping the house in elementary school, and by the time she was in high school was so busy cooking, cleaning and doing laundry that she missed most social activities. Her mother still insists she did no wrong, but obviously she loaded many of her burdens onto the tender shoulders of a child.

That case is an exception. Generally if there's error in households today it's in the opposite direction. Either Mom becomes the household servant, or the parents' bank account is drained to purchase the goods and services necessary to meet the family's expectations.

Regardless of how well off we become, some sharing of the load with children will help them for years to come. "Let me help you, Mommy" is the place to start, when the toddler is eager to help clean up or set the table. It takes a bit more time for us, but they learn best when they are willing.

My grandchildren, from the age of five or six, have pulled up a stool to the kitchen sink to work. Not hard, and not unsupervised, but enough to give them a sense of belonging and sharing.

This may seem rather stern to some, but with so many working parents today, the whole family needs to pull together for a smooth-running home. When done without shouting and threats, the result is an uncommonly peaceful home where harmony prevails and children become responsible, mature adults.

MEDITATION:

"Train up a child in the way he should go: and when he is old, he will not depart from it." Proverbs 22:6

ACTION STEPS:

❧ According to experts, by the age of two toddlers can pick up their own toys. After that they can help with light housework—dusting and stripping sheets off a bed are fun. Around seven or nine, depending on the child's agility, they can set the table for a meal and clear the dishes afterwards. At this age, we still have to take care of fine items ourselves. By the age of thirteen, they should have mastered the laundry, and even know how to iron. Cooking and needlework or sewing can start at early ages, under close supervision. The rule of thumb is, the earlier we start, the more it seems like fun instead of drudgery. We just have to be sensitive to when the children need to stop or skip chores altogether.

❧ What one child is ready for at a certain age doesn't mean another child can accomplish at the same age. How often we hear, "Your brother did this at your age; why can't you?" This undermines a child's confidence in himself, causes him to feel he has disappointed you, creates resentment and completely defeats the purpose of having him work alongside you. So keep those observations to yourself!

❧ Get some godly childrearing books or videos by one of the experts who are so helpful today, such as Dr. James Dobson. These make great baby shower gifts for the next generation. The Bible says the older women are to instruct the younger. Gently showing them how to raise their children is a valuable help only someone who is experienced can give—someone like you!

W I S E   W O R D S :

"Once you put your hand to the plough, you don't remove it until you get to the end of the row."

> Alice Paul
> Suffragist

"Opportunities are usually disguised by hard work, so most people don't recognize them."

> Ann Landers
> Advice columnist

Families:

W e are exhorted often to pray for loved ones, unsaved friends and acquaintances, spiritual and government leaders, laborers for new converts, the sick and afflicted, the depressed, and the hurting. These needs fill our prayer times to fulfill the Bible's commands. But there is another prayer to be mindful of, and that is the prayer for future generations of our own families.

I had never heard the term "born again" until my husband became a Christian. It did not mean anything to me for a long time—until the Holy Spirit started speaking to my own heart. I still didn't get it until I became a born-again Christian myself. Everything spiritual came alive to me then.

I came from a rather uncommunicative family and no one ever really talked about spiritual matters until both Edwin and I sent news of our conversions to family members. Then one day when Daddy was visiting us, he said offhandedly, "My sister, Seretha, carried her Bible around with her everywhere."

Something in me clicked at that. My Aunt Seretha died somewhere around 1910 when she was a teenager, many years before I was born. I believe, though, she must have been the shining light in our family who prayed for her brothers and sisters and their families. Could it be that she prayed for their children and grandchildren too?

Someone must have prayed for us if we received Christ. Who prayed for you? And for whom are you praying?

God is a generational God. He promised the patriarch, Abraham, that his descendants would be as numerous as the stars in the heavens. He had plans for them long before the first child, Isaac, was born.

God intends to take care of us today and tomorrow and for generations to come. We can be secure in that knowledge when we just pray!

MEDITATION:

"Pray all the time. Ask God for anything in line with the Holy Spirit's wishes. Plead with him, reminding him of your needs, and keep praying earnestly for all Christians everywhere." Ephesians 6:18 TLB

ACTION STEPS:

❧ Sometimes we make prayer into such a chore! We think we have to sit down and systematically go through our lists, or beg God for hours on end. There is much to be said for a lengthy time of prayer when we get certain things settled with the Lord. But there is also something to be said for the impromptu prayers we can pray right when we think of something. As people come to your mind today, whisper a prayer for them, or kneel down in your living room for just a few minutes to pray for someone you've never prayed for before.

❧ How concerned are you for the members of your family who don't know the Lord? I am constantly amazed at the people whose families are in terrible circumstances, but who complain and worry rather than pray! If you have an unsaved husband, child or grandchild, pray today without delay!

GREAT PRAYER WARRIORS:

"Pray specifically and you will get specific answers."
Jeanne Caldwell
Christian Author

"Begin to pray, remembering these simple words:
Good overcomes evil.
Light dispels darkness.
Life swallows up death.
The Lord will eventually win every victory for you."
Mary Jean Pidgeon
Christian Author

LET'S PRAY:

Father, teach me how to pray for my family. I ask You to direct me to pray daily for those who don't yet know Jesus as Savior and for each one who is struggling to know You as deliverer and restorer. I pray in Jesus' name. Amen.

Living a Finely Textured Life

Lifestyle:

POETIC LIVING

The picture in a national newspaper caught my eye. Three adorable little girls wearing women's dresses, hats and jewelry were seated outdoors at a table set with tea cups. The picture was so lovely that I drank it in for a few seconds before I looked at the article. I was surprised to discover it was written by my friend, Sandy.

On a sultry Virginia day, with restless grandchildren running underfoot, she decided to do what she had always wanted to do with her daughters—throw a tea party. She dressed them up in "fancy" clothes, threw a lacy tablecloth over a card table placed outdoors, and instantly had a party on her hands.

Once I read her story, I wasn't surprised at all. People like Sandy seem to have a knack for seeing the beauty in life, even on an otherwise dreary day. I was proud of her for doing what she'd always been too busy to do when her own children were small. Spontaneity is certainly part of poetic living.

My husband has a knack for spontaneity that has always cheered my routine way of living. "Come on, let's go to the parade!" he may rush in the house saying. Then we'll dash off to the boat parade and have a delightful time together.

Poetic living is not just for people who have a special gift for it. We can train ourselves to see and appreciate the beauty all around us. There's charm in presenting a single rosebud to a friend or placing it alone on a table. We can quiet the most rebellious child by preparing special food, serving it on china, and sitting down to eat and chat.

Look for the art and beauty around you today. Better yet, start a new habit of poetic living.

MEDITATION:

"You have let me experience the joys of life and the exquisite pleasures of your own eternal presence." Psalm 16:11 TLB

ACTION STEPS:

ک What are your possibilities for poetic living today? Do you have an extra half hour while running errands to stop at a bookstore or library and get a book of poetry? Then sit down with some tea tonight and read it.

ک Create beauty for others. Light a scented candle and sit down to write a thoughtful letter to a friend or relative who will cherish it for years to come. Or invite someone over to a candlelight dinner. It doesn't have to be romantic; any friend will enjoy such a treat.

ک Start to search out art in its best forms. Tune your radio to catch an opera. Go eat in a fancy restaurant that makes food as beautiful as it is delicious (the secret is to order just a salad, desert and beverage, or just the main entree)! Buy tickets today for the next symphony or play near you. Go to your favorite public statue and have a picnic beneath it. When was the last time you visited the local museum? The possibilities are endless—it's just up to you to make them happen!

TOLD YOU SO:

"It takes great passion and great energy to do anything creative...It's just got to be right. You can't do it without that passion."

Agnes De Mille
Choreographer

"Because I love
The iridescent shells upon the sand
Take forms as fine and intricate as thought."

Kathleen Raine
Poet

Atmosphere:

Note after harmonious note poured from my stereo. The Christian songs sung by gospel greats against a background of orchestral strength made the most beautiful Christian music I'd heard in a long time. My house seemed transformed into the front room of heaven as I basked in the luxurious surroundings of serenity and God's divine presence. My spirit seemed to enlarge and I became fully aware that this music was written under the inspiration of the Holy Spirit of God Himself.

Preparing for bed a few hours later, my house was once again just my house and routine was routine. Yet I was still under the influence of that wonderful music. Then it occurred to me. I don't have such experiences from watching television, so why don't I turn on music more often?

God has always put a premium on music, from singers in His temple to musicians who led armies into battle to music that soothed the troubled spirit. All the Psalms, the biggest book in the Bible, are actually words of songs written mostly by David.

"Make a joyful noise unto the Lord, all ye lands," Psalm 100 reads, "Come before his presence with singing."

Compare that to a study I read about television. It said that people often turn on the television when they are depressed, lonely or otherwise feeling bad. What researchers found out is that watching television makes people feel even *more* depressed, *more* lonely, and worse off than ever!

There really is no debate. It's time to turn off the TV and use our time to renew the song in our hearts!

MEDITATION:

"Whatever is worthy of reverence and is honorable and seemly, whatever is just, whatever is pure, whatever is lovely and lovable, whatever is kind and winsome and gracious, if there is any virtue and excellence, if there is anything worthy of praise, think on and weigh and take account of these things—fix your minds on them." Philippians 4:8 AMP

ACTION STEPS:

&. The old chorus is true: "Only one life, 'twill soon be past, only what's done for Christ will last." Think carefully about everything you put in your spirit today.

&. Try "fasting" from television one day each week. Keep the TV off all day and put music in its place. Let your spirit soar as you worship our wonderful Lord.

&. "Hear" these stanzas of "How Great Thou Art" and let them refresh you:

> O Lord my God when I in awesome wonder
> Consider all the worlds Thy hands have made.
> I see the stars, I hear the rolling thunder
> Thy power throughout the universe displayed.

Then sings my soul my Savior God to thee
How great Thou art, how great Thou art
Then sings my soul, my Savior God to thee
How great Thou art, how great Thou art.

When Christ shall come with shout of acclamation
To take me home what joy shall fill my heart
Then I shall bow in humble adoration
And there proclaim, my God, how great Thou art!

Stuart K. Hine[10]

🕊 The first time I felt inexpressible joy as a new Christian was shortly after my conversion, when Edwin and I attended a campmeeting. The attendees were singing heartily the great anthem, "He Lives":

I serve a risen Savior He's in the world today
I know that He is risen whatever men may say
I see His hand of mercy, I hear His voice of cheer
And just the time I need Him He's always near

He lives! He lives! Christ Jesus lives today.
He walks with me and talks with me
Along life's narrow way.
He lives! He lives! Salvation to impart.
You ask me how I know He lives
He lives within my heart.

Albert H. Ackley[11]

SHE SAID IT IN SONG:

"Mine eyes have seen the glory
Of the coming of the Lord
He is trampling out the vintage

Where the grapes of wrath are stored.
He hath loosed the fateful lightning
Of His terrible, swift sword;
His truth is marching on!"
Battle Hymn of the Republic

Julia Ward Howe[12]
Writer, Suffragist

LET'S PRAY:

Father, I rejoice in Your presence. Thank You for dwelling in me and blessing our home. Forgive me for neglecting You for television. You are the lifter of my soul and I draw close to You. I receive Your peace and blessing. In Jesus' name I pray. Amen.

Retiring:

I occasionally hear of someone who retires from a job to sit at home thinking there's nothing left to do. What nonsense!

What happens usually when people retire? We have a retirement party, take a two- or three-week trip, then what? I'll tell you what—there is no such thing as retirement in Christianity! Something is always ready for us to do in God's Kingdom.

Jesus said, "I was hungry and thirsty, naked and lonely, and you fed me and gave me something to drink. You clothed me and took care of my loneliness. You eased my discomfort as I lay in prison. When did you do this? When you took care of my brothers and sisters here on earth who were undergoing these hardships" (See Matthew 25:31-46).

Isn't there someone on your street who needs cheering up? Do you know a wife who is heartbroken over her husband's habits? What about the young girl who's in trouble and needs your wisdom to straighten her out? "What can I do?" is the hearts' cry of the saints.

After an absence of many years, I've run across old friends whose light is gone from their eyes. They "retired" not only in body, but also in spirit. What a mistake to let this indolence overtake you! Jesus puts no age limit on service to Him. Keep the outgiving light of God burning until the day He takes you home.

MEDITATION:

Matthew 25. As you read this chapter in your favorite Bible translation, allow His words to prompt you to action.

ACTION STEPS:

❧ The Bible says not to despise the day of small beginnings. That can also be interpreted to begin things on their lowest level. If you don't know where to start working for the Lord, call your church and ask about the needy. Depending on your talents, gifts and abilities, you might help in a variety of ways. You may be needed to give someone a ride to church or to the grocery store. You may work in the local food pantry for the needy. You might stay home for latchkey children to call you after school or when they're scared. You might even give a family their entire Christmas, or help feed the homeless at a street feeding.

❧ Hone your conversational skills. Listen to others until you hear their need. Then provide whatever you can to meet that need. For some, it's a confirmation that their children really will grow out of the stage they're in. For others, you may have a piece of wisdom or information to help them with their career. Whatever you do, when talking to others don't talk about yourself. Although your last surgery may be all important to the fact that you're alive today, no one really wants to hear the gory details! What do they want to do? Talk about themselves, of course! That's only human. So seize those opportunities to get them talking and meet their needs.

❧ Become neighborly. Don't let yourself fall into the trap of becoming the old woman on the street who doesn't want kids playing on her lawn. Those kids may need a ride to church to get saved. Your influence may change your neighbors' lives!

THOSE WHO NEVER QUIT:

"I am only one; but still I am one. I cannot do everything, but still I can do something; I will not refuse to do the something I can do."

Helen Keller
Author, Social
Activist

"When one door of happiness closes, another opens; but often we look so long at the closed door that we do not see the one which has been opened for us."

Helen Keller
Author, Social
Activist

LET'S PRAY:

Father, make Your ways my ways, direct my attention away from myself and help me see the needs around me. Thank You for using the gifts and talents You have given me to be a blessing to others. In Jesus' name I pray. Amen.

Continuing:

What is the will of God for you? My husband and I receive many letters on this subject: "I'm seeking God's will for my life" or "I'm depressed because God hasn't revealed His will for me." I believe in earnestly seeking God's will, but I also believe He orders our steps each day of our lives.

Sometimes those who write have felt called to the ministry, so they quit their jobs and are sitting home waiting for God to act. We did that—once! We would have starved had it not been for Edwin's mother. She gave us a small apartment and kept us in food. Our ministry went nowhere except to a few small, humble church meetings. So Edwin decided to fast and pray. He sequestered himself in a portion of our home and stayed there. Still nothing happened.

In an encounter with his mother one day, she said to him, "Edwin, there is a difference between a fast and a hunger strike. We cannot force God to act before His time."

Edwin saw the wisdom of her words, found a paying job, and before long—in God's time—he was in full-time ministry. In the meantime, he answered every call to preach that he could.

How do we find the will of God? We find it by rising in the morning, starting out with breakfast, and getting on with the tasks of that day. God always uses people who are actively engaged in normal, everyday activity.

Look at people from the Bible. Gideon was doing his job, threshing wheat, when God called him to lead the nation. Moses was tending sheep when he saw the burning bush. Deborah was an active judge when the call came to go into battle for her people. They were in action, not sitting around.

As we attend to our daily tasks, God is working out the intricate details of our lives. Believe it, and don't stop until you see it happen!

MEDITATIONS:

"In all your ways acknowledge Him, and He will direct your paths." Proverbs 3:6 MLB

"The path of the just is as a shining light, that shineth more and more unto the perfect day." Proverbs 4:18

"The steps of a good man [woman] are ordered by the Lord." Psalm 37:23

ACTION STEPS:

&- Some parts of God's will are "no-brainers": Helping our child in a difficult school assignment; keeping a home neat, clean and filled with peace; helping a neighbor in distress; participating in the activities of the church we faithfully attend; working on the relationships in our families.

&- Finding God's will can sometimes seem like a frustrating treasure hunt for an elusive pot of gold. But it's generally not so mysterious. As we grow in God's wisdom, if we operate within the parameters of that wisdom, we'll automatically be in God's will. Instead of seeking the end of a rainbow, seek the wisdom of God. He promised to give wisdom to us, if we just ask.

WISE WOMEN:

"People see God every day; they just don't recognize Him."
> Pearl Bailey
> Singer, Actress

"Obey your book of instructions (the Bible) and you will be kept body, soul and spirit by the power of God."
> Lilian B. Yeomans
> Physician

"God has a good plan already laid out for each of us, but we will never enjoy it unless our mind is renewed with the Word, which is His thoughts and ideas about things. When our mind is renewed with His Word, we think His thoughts and not our own."
> Joyce Meyer
> Christian Author

Success:

Barbara had not been able to have children, so she threw herself into her career and rose to top management in her company. But something was troubling her. Generally buoyant and happy, her bleak attitude at lunch puzzled me until she finally let it out.

"I feel so guilty about my career," she moaned.

I was shocked. "Oh, come on!" I blurted, "No one deserves success more than you. You've worked so hard!"

"But that's not how my old friends see it," she said sadly. "They talk behind my back, and accuse me that I've changed."

"You have changed, Barbara. You have more responsibilities now. They could have done the same as you, but they didn't."

"But now they imagine I think I'm better than them."

Barbara's working friends would have loved to be where Barbara was, but instead of rejoicing they allowed jealousy to influence their judgment, making her feel guilty for her success. It's petty, immature and just plain mean to tear down a friend instead of celebrating her success.

No one can please everyone. "Friends" who demand to be pleased are not friends at all. I tried pointing this out to Barbara, but she was so emotional I finally realized the best thing I could do was just listen and pray.

A few tormenting months later, the so-called friend who was her prime attacker did some very unfriendly things. Suddenly, Barbara saw through her and realized she was being manipulated because of this woman's fears and insecurities. Barbara silently bowed out of the friendship and soon had a new circle of friends who accepted her for who she was.

When we give our all, we can't worry about pleasing those who don't. We can't carry their guilt or insecurity for not doing as well.

MEDITATIONS:

"Love works no harm to one's neighbor, so love meets all the Law's requirements." Romans 13:10 MLB

"I can do all things in him who strengthens me." Philippians 4:13 RSV

ACTION STEPS:

❧ Success cannot be measured merely by outward accomplishments. At the height of Barbara's career, she was unsuccessful in friendships and it made her too miserable to enjoy her other blessings. If all you've done is climb in one area—socially, in your career, as a mother, or in your church—it may be time to work on other areas to be successful at life overall.

❧ Can you recognize your true friends? Who is building you up, holding you accountable, encouraging you, complimenting you, praying for you, counseling with you, loving you, being available to you, and rejoicing with you in your accomplishments? That person is your friend! The one who lies to you, hides things from you, attacks you, hangs up on you when you don't see things her way, makes fun of you, acts superior to you, and falsely accuses you is not your friend. They may call themselves friends, but if that's what they're like, it's time to walk away.

❧ When you are feeling discouraged, think on who God says you are. Dwelling on what others say will always bring you down. Choose instead to speak what the Scriptures say about you. Romans 8:37 declares, "I am more than a conqueror through Him Who loved me" (author's paraphrase). Repeat the Word aloud to yourself, pray the Word into your spirit, and break through the discouragement. Live fully in all God has for you.

WHAT'S THAT YOU SAY?

"Success can make you go one of two ways. It can make you a prima donna, or it can smooth the edges, take away the insecurities, let the nice things come out."

Barbara Walters
Television Reporter

"You may be disappointed if you fail, but you are doomed if you don't try."

Beverly Sills
Singer

$\mathscr{L}$eadership:

While I was visiting Canada, I read the cover article of a Christian magazine. The topic was women in church leadership. It was written by certain leaders and educators who argued their various points of view.

The son of a woman pastor said at one time he did not agree with his mother's leadership, but affirmed women in all other aspects of ministry. Years later he reversed his stand and now believes the Bible teaches that women can hold any office. Another point of view emphatically expressed by a woman and Christian educator was that women should not be pastors. Others gave biblical evidence they believed supported their conviction that women should not hold leadership positions at all—ever.

Many churches have been troubled in recent years by the debate whether to ordain women. Yet several great movements, such as the Salvation Army, have always ordained women and quietly avoided the turmoil. Historically, much of the Church was led by women in the late 1800's. But during the aftermath of World War I, most leadership positions became available to men only.

I have seen both men and women excel in leadership, in church, business and government. I have also seen both fail. My greatest concern is women who copy men, becoming masculine in an attempt to reach their goals.

Denying sexual identity is not the way to achieve God's plan. Our gender was designed by God to fit His purpose for our lives. Everything has its place. Women are equipped by God to suit the goals He has for us—*as women.*

To attempt to be something we were not intended to be is to stoop below God's plan. Whether ministering in church, mission work, business, the military, home, education or government—every woman has the responsibility to act like a woman. This won't stop the centuries-old debate, but it will help you become who God created you to be.

MEDITATIONS:

Biblical examples:

Deborah the prophetess and Jael the wife of Heber (Judges 4-6).

Queen Esther's story (Esther 1-10).

Abigail's story (1 Samuel 25).

ACTION STEPS:

&❧ To accept yourself takes soul-searching and prayer, especially if you've been caught up in trying to be something else. Get into the Word of God daily and spend time in prayer. This gives God the opportunity to help you come to grips with who you are.

&❧ Some women were tormented by older brothers or neighborhood bullies when they were children. Their experiences made them feel bad about being "a girl." If this is you, reject those words and live free! Prayerfully go back over all the memories of the jeers and sneers you received, rejecting each one and forgiving the perpetrator. You cannot simply reject their words without also forgiving them. Forgiveness releases our past but unforgiveness binds it to us. It may be necessary for you to make a list of the people who injured you and what they said, then pray through each incident. This will give you great peace and your act of forgiveness will open your heart to God to complete the work.

❦ Do something feminine today! Paint your nails or toes. Stand in your living room and try some ballet moves you learned as a girl. Wear something frilly under your clothes. No one else may know, but you will, and it will heighten your sense of womanhood and give you a good, godly pride in how He made you.

SHE SAID IT:

"When a woman behaves like a man, why can't she behave like a nice man?"

> Dame Edith Evans
> Actress

"To be somebody, a woman does not have to be more like a man, but has to be more of a woman."

> Sally E. Shaywitz
> Physician and
> Writer

"Whether women are better than men I cannot say—but I can say they are certainly no worse."

> Golda Meir
> Prime Minister,
> Israel

Caring:

Years ago, we had stirring missions conventions in our churches. One year the pastors and their wives gathered together to hear exciting reports from missionaries who were home. These missionaries hoped we would care enough to pledge financial support to spread the gospel in foreign lands.

At the beginning of the meeting, missionaries marched down the center aisle wearing the native dress of the countries where they ministered. One of them, "Daddy Simpson," had labored for many years in China and now, in his eighties, was home for good, with the doors of Communist China shut tightly behind him. He shuffled down the aisle, a slight, stooped figure in his long black Chinese coat and white leggings that matched his hair.

Stirring reports from the mission field quickly ate up the clock, but Daddy Simpson had still not spoken. Concerned about letting him have his turn and keeping us all too late, the leaders said, "Please, Brother Simpson, keep your remarks brief."

At last, Daddy Simpson stepped up to the lectern and we politely applauded. Then, in an electrifying moment, he boomed just one word: "CHINA!" It seemed his voice would shake the rafters, but we heard his heart breaking even louder. That one word seemed to hang in the air with the weight of a billion lost souls.

What a moment. The pastors and dignitaries fell to their knees in prayer and there wasn't a dry eye in the house. The cry of a man's heart was more eloquent than any message given that night.

I have often measured how much I care by that evening. When we care with all our hearts, we don't have to convince anyone. It's apparent.

MEDITATION:

"He told them, 'You are to go into all the world and preach the Good News to everyone, everywhere.'" Mark 16:15 TLB

ACTION STEPS:

❧ How do we begin to care for others? I think of Jesus crying out to the inhabitants of Jerusalem, "How often would I have gathered your children together, even as a hen gathereth her chickens under her wings, and ye would not!" (Matthew 23:37). Without His compassion coming through us, our selfishness and laziness can diminish our capacity for caring. A good prayer is to ask God to love others through us. With His compassion, caring is only natural.

❧ Missions is one of the most noble causes we can ever apply ourselves to. It's one of the few offerings we can give that has no chance of benefiting ourselves, and one of the few sacrifices in prayer of which we may never know the results. Fortunately, there's no age limit on giving and caring for missions. Missions-minded churches are always the strongest churches. And missions-minded people are always the most caring, compassionate, and loving.

Spinning
the
Situation

E I G H T

Procrastination:

I wrote four letters in one day last week—what a great feeling! One missive was an apology for not writing weeks earlier. Now, why did I procrastinate when I knew how relieved I would feel once I completed the task? I think three things can make procrastinators of anyone.

For one, we may feel we'll lose focus on the task at hand if we do something else for a moment. For example, I prefer to go through my bills and pay them all at the same time. So when I question something, do I call right then? No, I set it aside to call at a more convenient time, which of course never comes. The problem lingers in the back of my mind until I finally do it days later.

Secondly, we may convince ourselves the task takes longer than it really does. I can assume that writing a letter might take hours, when it really takes just minutes. A friend once put off filing his income taxes because he believed it would take too long and he would owe a lot of money.

"How are your taxes coming?" I asked after months of his admitted procrastination.

"Haven't got to 'em yet," he'd answer, until one day he bounded up to me with a huge smile. "I did it! It didn't take nearly as long as I thought, and I'm getting money back." He only received this good news when he stopped procrastinating.

Thirdly, we can make the task out to be terribly complex. I might put off looking something up at the library which I think is difficult. Then I stop by a library when I have a few minutes and discover that in a flash I have my answer from their computer system.

For whatever reason, procrastination makes us feel guilty and hinders good results. There is a line of sporting goods that has the slogan, "Just do it." When we adopt such a slogan personally, we have the satisfied feeling that we "just did it." The task completed is its own reward.

MEDITATION:

"Roll your work onto the Lord and your plans will be achieved." Proverbs 16:3 MLB

ACTION STEPS:

&❧ Without hesitating, spring up right now and do something you've put off. Write that letter; plant flowers in that ragged flower pot on your front doorstep; call that dear old aunt you've neglected; hose off that dirty walkway.

&❧ In the busy work of life, we can often lose sight of who we are or where we are going. Disorganization, lack of planning, and lack of goal-setting keep us from doing all we are capable of achieving. Consider where you are in life today and where you believe God created you to be. Set goals and then reach for them.

Take out a tablet and write headings on three pages: Things I Must Do, Things I Want To Do, Things To Buy. Go through each list and pray over each item, staying open for God to tell you what to cross out or add. Now go down the left margin and write numbers in order of importance. That completed, go down the left margin and write dates by which you hope to accomplish the tasks. Now consult that list every day as part of your devotional time with God. Ask Him to help you stay on track.

A goal is not a goal unless it has a date on it. Don't forget that step!

🐦 Rejoice! Don't get morose over all that is left undone, but be thankful and rejoice over all you have accomplished today, this week, or this year.

THEY DID IT:

"The future is made of the same stuff as the present."
Simone Weil
Writer

"It is not fair to ask of others what you are not willing to do yourself."
Eleanor Roosevelt
Writer,
Humanitarian,
U. N. Delegate,
First Lady

Activity:

DO ALL THINGS

I just read about a seventy-year-old woman mountain climbing in Switzerland. When her guide divided the hikers into fast and slow groups, he put her with the fast. Her vigor and stamina outlasted those half her age. Reading such a story, I believed this woman tackled all of life with that kind of energy.

Contrast her to the sedentary woman whose inactivity dulls her zest for living and creates a depressing air for those around her. The sedentary woman's routine robs others of the contributions she could have made and ultimately becomes her death—mentally, physically and spiritually. First goes spontaneity, then personality and cheerfulness, then energy and health.

I plead guilty on all counts. Fortunately, my husband keeps a young man's schedule which keeps me on my toes. Activity, even if it's just an active mind, produces energy which will keep us producing, contributing, and making a difference for others.

Robert Fulton's active mind wondered what made steam as he watched a kettle of water boil. As a result he invented the steam engine, which revolutionized the country and launched the Industrial Revolution. A man in a recent news report had crippling arthritis, yet he had an idea that physical limitations could not quench. All that moved in his whole body were just two fingers, and with them he typed out his first novel—and then found a publisher for it!

When our minds, bodies or spirits stagnate we lose energy which causes lost strength, resulting in a shortened life—which robs our family and community of our contributions. Our experiences and all we have learned is far too important to waste in sedentary, dormant living.

When we stay active, moving our bodies, exercising our minds and feeding our spirits, we increase and enhance our lives and the lives of those around us.

MEDITATION:

"Take delight in the Lord, and he will give you the desires of your heart. Commit your way to the Lord; trust in him, and he will act." Psalm 37:4,5 RSV

ACTION STEPS:

❧ Are you stagnant in spirit? I realize we are not all evangelists, but we can certainly be ready to give someone an answer about our faith when they ask for it. When someone asks, "What makes you tick? What is this warmth I feel about you?" We need to be ready to have the right answer. When God's Word is alive in us and our spirits are active, we have the answer.

❧ Your local library has how-to books on just about anything you could want to do, so you can try something without a monetary investment. Educational television also can teach you how to build a house, how to be a great fisherman and many other subjects. Or you can buy whole series of books or tapes to learn another language. What have you got to lose in reactivating yourself, except some weight or wasted hours?

1 2 S T E P S · F O R · L I F E ©¹³:

The following steps to increase an active life span are given by Dr. Kenneth Cooper of The Cooper Institute for Aerobics Research, who coined the term "aerobics."

Stop illegal drug use and abstain or limit alcohol consumption

Terminate smoking and smokeless tobacco

Exercise regularly (at least thirty minutes three times per week) and sleep six to eight hours each night

Pursue and maintain ideal body weight

Supplement your diet with calcium and the antioxidants vitamin C, vitamin E and beta carotene

Fasten safety belts

Obtain good prenatal health care

Regularly have medical check-ups and perform self-exams

Limit animal fats, cholesterol and sodium in your diet

Immunize preschoolers and senior citizens (polio, tetanus, mumps, diphtheria, measles, rubella, and whooping cough vaccines for preschoolers; pneumonia, flu and tetanus vaccines for senior citizens)

Forbid excessive sun exposure or wear sun block

Eat more fresh vegetables and fruit, high fiber goods, whole grains and drink more water

SAY IT AGAIN:

"When you cease to make a contribution you begin to die."

Eleanor Roosevelt
Writer,
Humanitarian,
U. N. Delegate,
First Lady

"This became a credo of mine…attempt the impossible in order to improve your work."

Bette Davis
Actress

Career Change:

DREAMS COME TRUE

Aching, yearning, frustrated. This is not a cold medicine commercial, but the description of many working women who juggle a job and family, all the while dreaming of a different career.

A mother's ideal is to be with her children, yet many must work outside jobs. But it seems that most who work aspire to something else. I have read that 85 percent of workers want a different profession. They wish they could write the greatest novel, train to become a marathon runner, study to become a Bible scholar, rise to the presidency of the company or do other exciting things.

I believe you *can* make dreams happen, and not at the expense of your children. God puts desires in our hearts to motivate us to accomplish them. What better lesson can you give your children, young or old, than to let them see you pursue your dreams and excel in the areas in which God has gifted you? If we want our children to pursue God's best for their lives instead of sliding through life, settling for the dictates of circumstance, then we must show them how.

A friend of mine was widowed early and forced to take a dead-end clerical job to support her family. Unwilling to waste her mind and desires, as a single mother she plugged away in night classes year after year while three children went through high school. By the time the children were grown, she graduated.

Today she owns her own business and all three children went to college, following in her footsteps.

Another friend now works with abused women and children. She always wanted to attend college but decided to wait until her children left home. One thing after another detained her, but she finally graduated. When she crossed that platform to receive her degree, she was sixty-three!

Too often our wishes make us want to escape today and live in tomorrow. The truth is, tomorrow is an illusion. We only have today. We're not fictional characters with unlimited years to find ourselves. We're not practicing life, we're living it.

So get going today. Don't waste time! Your dreams can come true.

MEDITATION:

"Be careful how you act; these are difficult days. Don't be fools; be wise: make the most of every opportunity you have for doing good. Don't act thoughtlessly, but try to find out and do whatever the Lord wants you to." Ephesians 5:15-17 TLB

ACTION STEPS:

❧ In my book *The Unique Woman*, I advised working mothers to utilize their time out of the house to the maximum. In other words, if you have to leave your children for ten hours a day, at least make as much money as you can while you are away! If you are able to attend classes to make a better life for your family, why not put your nose to the grindstone and work until you make it happen.

You don't have to do it at the expense of your family. If they spend time with their homework and hobbies, you can be studying nearby. Your children will appreciate you for your sacrifice. The few years of hard work is not much compared to the length of your life, especially when you consider how much more you will be able to contribute. Even my friend at sixty-three has perhaps ten or twenty years to pour into others before age takes its toll.

❧ You *do* have alternatives. When I rode a bus to work I crocheted a quilt for my son and daughter-in-law. When I drove a car to work I avoided freeways and drove beautiful routes down country roads. God's universe lifted my spirit, bringing praise to my lips for such a wonderful Savior. Look at your alternatives today and see how you can capitalize on your time and resources.

❧ Have you always regretted not going to college? Take immediate advantage of the proliferation of community colleges to get yourself started. Study and plan. My daughter did four years in three, cutting out an entire year of tuition. Strategize, set goals, then get busy! It will be over before you know it and, unlike doing your hair or cooking dinner, once accomplished, it is behind you forever.

❧ The library is full of books and videos on every subject imaginable. When you are motivated with God's power helping you and His Spirit leading you, it's surprising how you can make time on your lunch hour, breaks, during the ride to and from work, or after the kids are in bed to research your dreams. Learn all you can, then pursue until you reach your goals.

FROM ONE WHO KNOWS:

"The future belongs to those who believe in the beauty of their dreams."

> Eleanor Roosevelt
> Writer,
> Humanitarian,
> U. N. Delegate,
> First Lady

LET'S PRAY:

Father, only You know what I can accomplish with Your inspiration. I'm ready to go forward to achieve Your vision for me. I commit my way to You and trust You to direct me. Nothing is impossible with You. In Jesus' name I pray. Amen.

Overcoming:

Women who overcome severe circumstances arouse my greatest admiration. My friend, Nan, lived her entire married life with a husband who fell far short of the ideal. Like Abigail's husband Nabal, Nan's husband was unloving, selfish, unmindful of his marriage vows, and his immaturity led to a rocky work record.

Those of us who knew them marveled at Nan's perseverance, her constantly forgiving attitude, and her sincere devotion to God. Some advised Nan to leave her husband, quoting her the scriptural grounds for divorce. Yet Nan stood firm, doing her best at home and supporting her family by working at a clerical job. She managed to raise four outstanding children, yet in her forties she seemed destined to struggle the rest of her life.

Then seemingly out of the blue, she took a sales course and landed a job on the bottom rung of a national company. After years of developing strong character at home she fell into sales like a seasoned pro. "No" merely meant to work harder. Disgruntled customers just required a smile and encouragement. Interoffice jealousies brought out balm for hurt feelings. Clerical "dirty" work did not phase her. She handled details like a breeze. In ten years she was the number one salesperson nationwide!

With her new status, her husband became more attentive. Now they enjoy each other's company and vacation together all over the world. They are also building their dream house for their retirement. If you didn't know them, you would think they had lived in bliss for thirty years!

If anyone had reason to divorce, to blame her difficulties on someone else and to run from her problems, Nan did. Yet she caught her second wind and made her life a success by building character, maintaining a forgiving attitude, and honoring God. In return, God has generously honored Nan.

MEDITATION:

"For the man who uses well what he is given shall be given more, and he shall have abundance." Matthew 25:29 TLB

ACTION STEPS:

🐦 Have you ever read *The Greatest Salesman in the World* by Og Mandino? Regardless of whether or not you are a salesman, read aloud his ten steps for success. He recommends you read them every day to see a change in your life and attitude:

1. Failure will no longer be my payment for struggle.

2. I will greet this day with love in my heart.

3. I will persist until I succeed.

4. I am nature's greatest miracle.

5. I will live this day as if it is my last.

6. Today I will be master of my emotions.

7. I will laugh at the world.

8. Today I will multiply my value a hundredfold.

9. I will act now.

10. I will pray for guidance.[14]

THINK ABOUT IT:

"Far away there in the sunshine are my highest aspirations. I may not reach them, but I can look up and see their beauty, believe in them and try to follow where they lead."

> Louisa May Alcott
> Writer

"Character contributes to beauty. It fortifies a woman as her youth fades. A mode of conduct, a standard of courage, discipline, fortitude and integrity can do a great deal to make a woman beautiful."

> Jacqueline Bisset
> Actress

Handicaps:

Even from my short height, I could see that Uncle Jim's gray mustache matched his gray and white hair way at the top of his tall, slender body. To my child's eye he was one of the biggest men alive, and as I look back, he still is.

For many summers Mother packed me and my sister off to Great Uncle Jim and Great Aunt Til's farm in Vermont. What an education for two little city girls! We loved the adventure of living without electricity, hot water and indoor plumbing. I was enthralled with farm life—feeding chickens, jumping off the barn beam into sweet-smelling hay, helping Aunt "Til" (Matilda Jane) pick vegetables and fruit from the gardens and orchard, cleaning the oil lamps—I even learned how to pluck and clean chickens!

Most of all, I was fascinated by Uncle Jim's hands. Without Mother there to correct me, I felt I could stare all I wanted and I did. Where there should have been fingers there was almost nothing. Frostbite had taken all eight fingers when he worked as a young man on the Canadian railroad. Fortunately he had his thumbs. On one hand he had just enough stump of a forefinger to be able to hold things, and on the other he had finger stumps. With those hands he worked a good portion of his 360-acre farm.

Every morning at 4:00 he started his daily chores by milking the cows. In late summer, he would hitch his ill-tempered horse,

Bess, to the mower and mow the hay that would feed the animals during the long winter months. Once a week he would hitch Bess to the old buckboard wagon. We'd scramble up beside him for the six-mile drive to town to trade eggs and milk for needed supplies. In town nobody stared at Uncle Jim's hands. He was just Jim Hill to them and they took him for who he was, never mind his handicaps.

When I meet people who make a success in spite of their physical limitations, I can see in them the determination and the twinkle in their eyes that I watched in Uncle Jim. He was always working against the odds and winning every day. Uncle Jim was and always will be a hero to me.

MEDITATION:

"I have strength for all things in Christ Who empowers me—I am ready for anything and equal to anything through Him Who infuses inner strength into me, [that is, I am self-sufficient in Christ's sufficiency]." Philippians 4:13 AMP (Also see I Samuel 17:32,50)

ACTION STEPS:

❧ You can live in the "If only's"—if only I could see better, walk better, do sports better, know more, have more talent, express myself better—or you can accept what you have. With God's help you can work to enhance the abilities and talents He gave you. If you adjust your thinking about who you are and what you can do, you may be surprised at your success.

❧ Fold a piece of paper lengthwise. Title the top of the first column "CAN DO" and the second "NEED WORK." Then list the things you can do well in the first column, and in the next column those you can do a little but need work. (There is no column for what you cannot do at all.)

Using the first column as a reference list, make sure you utilize and maximize one item from the "CAN DO" list every day. Go to those strengths, rather than frustrating yourself with your weaknesses.

Create a plan for your NEED WORK list. Take classes, practice, read or seek help to turn your NEED WORK list into a CAN DO list. As you develop new talents, move the NEED WORK items to the CAN DO side and add something else to the NEED WORK list.

As you grow, you'll discover more latent talents which may get their start on the NEED WORK list. While your CAN DO list grows, your NEED WORK list will too, causing you to continue improving yourself and strengthening your own self-confidence.

WORTH SAYING:

"Aerodynamically, the bumble bee shouldn't be able to fly, but the bumble bee doesn't know it so it goes on flying anyway."
Mary Kay Ash
Businesswoman

"I may be compelled to face danger, but never fear it, and while our soldiers can stand and fight, I can stand and feed and nurse them."
Clara Barton
Nurse, Founder of
the American
Red Cross

Aging:

KEEP THE FAITH

Everyone wants to age gracefully. We buy creams, study magazines, and visit salons and doctors to keep ourselves as fit and good-looking as we can for as long as we can. Yet many of us have overlooked the most obvious place to start—from the inside out.

My friend Patti had a stroke as a young woman and has gone to doctors all her life to overcome the numbness down one side of her body. She has learned to walk again, to get out of a chair and to bend over to work in her garden. But when you meet her, you never even see her physical limitations. All you see is her shining face.

The Bible clearly says not to worry about the outside, the adorning of our bodies, but to develop a sweet spirit that is much more beautiful. How true that is! I have met many women who had the privilege of seeing the best plastic surgeons and buying the best clothes at the most exclusive stores, but they don't hold a candle to Patti. She outshines them all with her radiant, loving spirit.

With Jesus Christ at the center of our lives, we are tapped into His peace, His power to overcome problems and His promise of "abundant life." The more we accept of Him, the more radiant we become. And the older we are, the more time we have to bring Him into our lives!

MEDITATIONS:

"Don't be concerned about the outward beauty that depends on jewelry, or beautiful clothes, or hair arrangement. Be beautiful inside, in your hearts." 1 Peter 3:3,4 TLB

"They that wait upon the Lord shall renew their strength." Isaiah 40:31

ACTION STEPS:

❧ Live it up and visit the make-up counter at your favorite department store if you want, but also spend time with your Bible and the Lord (and a book like this!) every morning.

❧ The Bible is described as "living water." If a face freshly splashed with cold water makes us look alive again, think what happens when we splash our spirits with the living water of the Word. It might not seem like anything as you read day after day. But God promises His Word will not return void, which means it will eventually all add up. Ingesting the Word is like ingesting life itself. You cannot help but gain!

❧ There's no rule that says an older woman has to look frumpy. Instead of falling prey to a lack of imagination, get some fashion magazines and look at the pictures to get an idea of what's happening today. Update yourself! You'll feel better and look better too.

THEY SHOULD KNOW:

"So much has been said and sung of beautiful young girls, why don't somebody wake up to the beauty of old women?"

Harriet Beecher Stowe
Writer

"Memory is history recorded in our brain, memory is a painter, it paints pictures of the past and of the day."

> Grandma Moses
> (Anna Mary Robertson
> Moses)
> Painter

JUST FOR FUN:

"Old age is like a plane flying through a storm. Once you're aboard, there's nothing you can do."

> Golda Meir
> Prime Minister, Israel

Physical Threads

Threads

N I N E

Weight:

So Much To Gain

What an adjustment I had last year when Edwin and I moved from our urban digs to a somewhat rural neighborhood. I realized just how different it was when I discovered what most people in our country already knew about—discount department stores. What great bargains one can find there! The first time I saw low prices on everything from light bulbs to tennis shoes I was hooked.

But frequenting those nearby stores has brought me to an uncomfortable awareness. It seems like standing in every line, and walking down every aisle, are overweight women. What a shame to see otherwise beautiful women carrying around as much as a hundred pounds of extra weight. Besides making themselves unhappy—and making others sad to see them—their extra weight is very hard on their health.

In our society we have an abundance of food, but we don't need to eat it all! At times I find it easy to let myself go and consume a great deal, such as during holiday seasons. The weight is so easy to put on and so hard to take off, particularly if we don't tackle it right away. There were times when I could hardly wait to get my hands on a chocolate chip cookie or a lemon square, but looking at myself in a mirror stopped me (most of the time anyway!).

Choosing healthful foods is a difficult decision to make, but the results give major satisfaction. Often we must not look at what we give up, but what we receive. One man I know looked at a piece of pizza one day and said, "I want Jesus, not you, to rule my life!" He set it back down and during the next year he lost eighty-five pounds.

Fill your life with other interests besides food. Ask God to help you. Trust Him. He will help you achieve the ideal weight and healthy body you need to live a rich and satisfying life.

And when you see those chocolates on sale—skip over to the next aisle and stock up on light bulbs instead!

MEDITATION:

"Put a knife to your throat if you are a man (woman) given to appetite." Proverbs 23:2 RSV

ACTION STEPS:

&. But you say, "I can't diet." All right, don't diet, but instead of eating too much every meal, use a bit of restraint. I recently read that our stomachs can only handle two fistfuls of food at a time. Eat about that much, until you are barely full, then quit!

&. Learn the habits of successful dieters:

Rest your fork between every bite.

Set up a place where you will eat, go there three times each day, and never eat in between, except for low calorie snacks.

Put all signs of food out of sight.

Quit watching television (or watch only programs with no food advertisers).

Reorganize your cupboards and refrigerator so only healthy foods are handy.

🍂 Go to one of those booths at a fair or tourist attraction where you can have a picture made of your face inside someone else's body. Choose a skinny body, then tack that picture up somewhere to serve as a constant reminder of how you want to look!

🍂 Change the way you eat to limit yourself to mostly fat-free, low-calorie foods. Or, make a chart of the prescribed food exchanges and limit yourself daily to consume them only.

🍂 Get some form of exercise every day, even if it's just a walk around the park or a good stretch all over your body before you go to bed.

FOOD FOR THOUGHT:

"You are free up to the point of choice, then your choice controls your future."

Mary Crowley
Author

Exercise:

I was startled one day when I heard Bob Schuller on his "Hour of Power" telecast say, "I was so tired yesterday, I had to get out and jog four miles." Then he said he felt much better. Four miles! I'd be half dead, or at the least ready for four days of bed rest!

Still, I understood his point. Fatigue saps the oxygen from our bones, joints and minds. A good workout puts back into the body much of the oxygen lost through fatigue. My "good workout" does not mean I go to the gym to lift weights. No way! I'm not talking about head-rattling, muscle-pulling, energy-defying exercise. That's wonderful for some, but not for me.

What's practical for me is a good walk. I used to walk two miles easily, but now ten minutes is comfortable. Doing that daily, or at least three or four times a week, helps oxygenate our bodies. What's important is to increase our heart rate, usually until we break out in a little sweat.

Exercise is a natural tranquilizer. It's also the best antidote to stress and tension. When we exercise, we release endorphins into the bloodstream that give us a sense of well-being. That sounds like just the ticket for me!

Regular exercise has so much to offer—it lowers our blood pressure, reduces cholesterol, and to top it off, makes our problems seem smaller! I take it even a step further. I use the minutes

I walk for talking with the Lord. Only when I'm out walking am I sure no one will interrupt me, even by telephone.

With so much to gain, why not start exercising today!

MEDITATION:

"Do you not know that your body is a temple of the Holy Spirit within you, whom you have from God, and that you do not belong to yourselves?" 1 Corinthians 6:19 MLB

ACTION STEPS:

❧ If you're trying to diet, there's nothing like exercise to make that weight come off. Although walking is great, many people find variety necessary to keep them interested in their exercise program. Many videos today target maturing women. If you have a VCR, that might be just what you need to spice up your routine. And videos allow you to exercise year round. No excuses! Start today.

❧ If walking is your choice, there's many helpful audio cassettes and clubs that can help you. A light-weight cassette player may be a big investment for some, but it might be just what you need to stay active. The nonstop music and tips by trained instructors really help. Try your local department stores for a good variety. Also, try your local walking club. They are so popular these days—you just may make a lot of friends while you're at it!

FOOD FOR THOUGHT:

"If the first woman God ever made was strong enough to turn the world upside down all alone, these women together ought to be able to turn it back, and get it right side up again!"

> Sojourner Truth
> Suffragist,
> Abolitionist

"A turtle makes progress when it sticks its neck out."

> Anonymous

"If we short-circuit our physical lives through lack of care, then of necessity we short-circuit what God desires for our spiritual lives."

> Margaret Hicks
> Christian Author

Menopause:

Meagan is a remarkable woman. But when she became pregnant at forty, she didn't believe the symptoms. Her mother suggested she was going through "the change." A friend said it sounded like she had a tumor. Frightened by either option, Meagan finally saw her doctor. Sure enough, she was pregnant—*very* pregnant by then—four months along!

Meagan's friend Shirley didn't seem that much older than Meagan. Their teenaged daughters were friends. But one day Shirley realized something was wrong. She checked with her doctor and he confirmed that she was going through menopause.

During that ephemeral time between childbearing years and old age, when you feel too old for one but too young for the other, menopause comes—a change in our bodies from one life cycle to another.

For some women, the shift from one stage of life to another is accompanied by uncomfortable symptoms such as hot flashes, night sweats, irritability, depression, and an overwhelming desire to get rid of their husbands. According to one researcher, such problems didn't matter much to previous generations until we started living so long. But that still doesn't help us.

I have a theory for our emotional changes at menopause. Besides the hormonal changes, I believe our emotions respond to the knowledge that our childbearing years have ended. If that's true, perhaps depression can be alleviated by viewing it as a positive, not a negative. Shirley will never be in Meagan's shoes again. And there is freedom in that!

For everything we go through during menopause, we do well to find a way to celebrate the changes God is making—and look forward to the next fifty years of life.

MEDITATION:

"The Lord will perfect that which concerneth me: thy mercy, O Lord, endureth for ever." Psalm 138:8

ACTION STEPS::

❧ Many women become frustrated with their husbands and families when menopause sets in. Remember the verse, "It came to pass." This too shall pass, so ride it out! Don't do anything drastic. The best years of life are yet to come.

❧ Use all the discipline you've learned during the first half of your life to discipline your mind. Weed your thought life every day like you would a perfect garden, and keep all the negatives out.

❧ Use the first morning minutes, after waking but before rising, to program your mind and day. Choose what you will do today. Make a deal with yourself on your thought life. Make goals, and if you reach your goals, line up a special treat—a long distance phone call, a bubble bath, or the luxury of reading your favorite magazine.

FOOD FOR THE SOUL:

"The delights of self-discovery are always available."

Gail Sheehy
Writer

"You don't get to choose how you're going to die, or when. You can only decide how you're going to live. Now!"

Joan Baez
Singer, Songwriter

Resurrection:

The most cherished holiday of a Christian's year is Easter, the celebration of the resurrection, the day Jesus rose from the dead and gave us the gift of eternal life.

Although I like to think of Jesus riding into Jerusalem to a cheering crowd on Palm Sunday, a few days later the same crowd jeered Him and demanded He be crucified. However, when I think of the horrors of the crucifixion, I know Resurrection Day is right around the corner!

I love to meditate on the resurrection, the cornerstone of our faith. We celebrate with lavenders, pinks and yellows, and buy that special dress. We buy potted lilies and wear a corsage. We make Easter baskets, exchange candy or gifts, and go to church as a family. Then we celebrate that Jesus rose triumphantly from the grave as He promised, breaking through the barriers of death so we could live forever.

This past Easter was like a spiritual shot of vitamins for me. After all these years, I am only now beginning to get a glimmer of what it means to follow Christ. Some people seem to understand and accept it so easily. They seem to radiate the life of Christ and always leave me with a sense of awe. But I am just beginning to understand that *every day is a resurrection day in the life of a believer!*

The more we know Him, the better it gets, building in wonder and awe, growing in knowledge and wisdom, and experiencing more and more the unfathomable depth of His love. One day we will finally see Him face to face, but in the meantime, we can have the joy of knowing what Jesus Christ did for us on Easter—every day of our lives here on earth.

MEDITATION:

"That I may know him, and the power of his resurrection." Philippians 3:10

ACTION STEPS:

🍃 To celebrate Christ's resurrection today, do something to rejoice, even if it's the wrong season. Put fresh flowers on your table. Give someone a gift as a reminder of God's gift to us!

SING IT:

Lo in the grave He lay, Jesus my Savior
Waiting the coming day, Jesus my Lord
Up from the grave He arose
With a mighty triumph o'er His foes
He arose a victor of the dark domain
And He lives forever with His saints to reign.
He arose! He arose!
Hallelujah, Christ arose!
Christ Arose

Robert Lowry[15]

JUST THINK OF IT:

"We are on a journey, and our destination is Heaven."
Margaret Hicks
Christian Author

LET'S PRAY:

Father, I praise You for the boundless future we have received by Your hand and through the life of our Lord Jesus Christ, the Messiah! I am born again to an everlasting hope, through the resurrection of Jesus from the dead. I have an imperishable inheritance in heaven, infinitely more precious than gold. May Your will be accomplished in my life and Your glory fill the earth. Thank You for Your incomparable love and matchless mercy. In Jesus' name. Amen.

A Final Word

Heavenly Father, I pray those who read this book and do not know of Your marvelous plan of salvation through the life, death and resurrection of Your Son, the Lord Jesus Christ, will find that life today as they read these words:

Dear Lord, forgive me of all the sins I have committed against You. I believe Your Son, Jesus Christ, died for me and I accept Him now as my Lord and Savior. Help me always to put You first in my life. And when I die, take me to heaven where I may dwell with You always. Amen.

Endnotes

1. Christina Rossetti, *Poetical Works of Christina Rossetti* (New York: Macmillan, 1904), 314.

2. Emily Dickinson, *The Complete Poems of Emily Dickinson* (Boston: Little, Brown & Company, 1890), 668.

3. Edna St. Vincent Millay, *Collected Poems: Edna St. Vincent Millay* (New York: Harper & Row, 1917), 127.

4. Helen Jackson, *Sonnets & Lyrics* (Temecula, CA: Reprint Services Corp., 1992), 230.

5. Emily Jane Brönte, *Emily Jane Brönte: The Complete Poems* (New York: Penguin Books, 1992), 196.

6. Kenneth W. Osbeck, *Amazing Grace: 366 Inspiring Hymn Stories for Daily Devotions*, "I Surrender All," Judson W. Van De Venter (1855-1939), (Grand Rapids, MI: Kregel Publications, 1990), 261.

7. Emily Dickinson, *The Complete Poems of Emily Dickinson*, 658.

8. Ibid., 433

9. Amy Lowell, *The Poems of Amy Lowell* (Boston: Houghton Mifflin Company, 1912), 2-3.

10. Kenneth W. Osbeck, *Amazing Grace: 366 Inspiring Hymn Stories for Daily Devotions*, "How Great Thou Art," words by Stuart K. Hine, 141; copyright © 1953, renewed 1981 by Manna Music, Inc., Valencia, CA.

11. Ibid., "He Lives," Albert H. Ackley, 128; copyright © 1933 by The Rodeheaver Company (div. of Word, Inc.).

12. Ibid., "Battle Hymn of the Republic," Julia Ward Stowe, (1862).

13. "12 STEPS-FOR-LIFE," copyright © Dr. Kenneth Cooper, The Cooper Institute for Aerobics Research; Dallas, Texas.

14. Og Mandino, *The Greatest Salesman in the World* (Hollywood, FL: Bantam Books, 1968); published with permission by Frederick Fell, Inc.; "Step 1," 52; "Step 2," 58; "Step 3," 63; "Step 4," 68; "Step 5," 73; "Step 6," 78; "Step 7," 83; "Step 8," 88; "Step 9," 93; "Step 10," 100.

15. Kenneth W. Osbeck, *Amazing Grace: 366 Inspiring Hymn Stories for Daily Devotions*, "Christ Arose," Robert Lowry (1874).

Quote Acknowledgments

I acknowledge and thank the following people for the quotes used in this book: Kathleen Norris (19), Louise Nevelson (19), Beverly Sills (24,203), Dorothy Parker (24), Kay Lyons (26), Pearl S. Buck (26,33,37,173), Bette Davis (26,220), Jeannette Rankin (29), Adrienne Rich (37), Fanny Brice (37), Katherine Graham (41), Anne Frank (41,127), Barbara Walters (41,203), Lucille Ball (42), Ingrid Bergman (46), Emily Dickinson (46,121,140), Helen Keller (49,89,195), Edith Armstrong (49,109), Georgia O'Keefe (59), Mother Teresa (59), Amelia Earhart (64), Abigail Van Buren (64,131), Lillian Hellman (67), Jeannie Caldwell (67,181), Colette (71), Louisa May Alcott (76,113,227), Erma Bombeck (81,92), Jean Kerr (81), Martha Graham (86), Eleanor Roosevelt (86,136,153,161,169,215,220,224), Marie Curie (89,140), Joyce Meyer (92,95,99,199), Dinah Shore (95), Queen Victoria (95), Linda Asbury (99), Louise Bogan (103), Edwin Louis Cole (109), Mary Kay Ash (109,231), Golda Meir (117,207,235), Anne Morrow Lindbergh (121), Virginia Woolf (127), Virginia Graham (128), Sarah Caldwell (131), Mahalia Jackson (131), Phyllis McGinley (135), Fanny Kemble (144), Agatha Christie (144), Edna O'Brien (147), Alice Marble (148), Emma Hart Willard (153), Margaret Mead (157), Annie Sullivan (157), Lillian Carter (161), Sandra Day O'Connor (165), Olga Masters (165), Berenice Abbott (169), Billy Jean King (174), Alice Paul (177), Ann Landers (177), Mary Jean Pidgeon (181), Agnes De Mille (187), Kathleen Raine (187), Pearl Bailey (199), Lilian B. Yeomans, M.D. (199), Dame Edith Evans (207), Sally E. Shaywitz (207), Simone Weil (215), Jacqueline Bisset (227), Clara Barton (231), Harriet Beecher Stowe (234), Grandma Moses (235), Mary Crowley (241), Sojourner Truth (245), Margaret Hicks (245,253), Gail Sheehy (249), Joan Baez (249)

About the Author

Nancy Corbett Cole has raised three outstanding children and is integrally involved in ministry with her husband. Concurrently, she has been involved extensively in church activities and served on the leadership committee of several ministries. She has cohosted and been a featured vocalist on two Emmy award-winning television programs.

Mrs. Cole served in the U.S. Coast Guard. She is currently an officer for the board of Directors of Edwin Louis Cole Ministries, is also involved in various civic groups, and has been a guest at the White House in both church and government-related capacities. She has ministered throughout the world as a featured speaker and with her husband. Her special interests include being an active grandmother and giving of herself regularly to help the disadvantaged and widowed.

Other Books by
Nancy Corbett Cole

The Unique Woman

Tapestry of Life

You can contact Mrs. Cole at the following address:

Edwin Louis Cole Ministries
International Headquarters
P.O. Box 610588
Dallas, Texas 75261

This and other books available at your local bookstore.

Honor Books
Tulsa, Oklahoma